"*The Great Vegan Grains Book* is not only informative, but full of deliciously unique and beautifully photographed recipes that are sure to become a fixture in your meal lineup! Celine and Tami share their immense knowledge of grains in a fun, casual, and incredibly tasty way."

—**Rose Weitzner, M.D.**, managing director of the Vegan Trade Council

"In their new book, Celine and Tami show you that in order to add whole grains to your diet you don't have to stop at oatmeal or brown rice. *The Great Vegan Grains Book* is packed with mouthwatering and unique, often internationally inspired, recipes that will take you on a fantastic journey to explore the amazing world of amaranth, quinoa, spelt, and other wonderful seeds and cereals."

—**Constanze Reichardt**, founder of seitanismymotor.com

Quarto is the authority on a wide range of topics.

Quarto educates, entertains and enriches the lives of our readers—enthusiasts and lovers of hands-on living.

www.QuartoKnows.com

First published in the United States of America in 2016 by
Fair Winds Press, an imprint of
Quarto Publishing Group USA Inc.
100 Cummings Center
Suite 406-L
Beverly, Massachusetts 01915-6101
Telephone: (978) 282-9590
Fax: (978) 283-2742
QuartoKnows.com
Visit our blogs at QuartoKnows.com

20 19 18 17 16   1 2 3 4 5

ISBN: 978-1-59233-699-9

Digital edition published in 2016
eISBN: 978-1-62788-826-4

Library of Congress Cataloging-in-Publication Data available

Book and cover design by Megan Jones Design
Book layout by Megan Jones Design
Photography by Celine Steen (www.celinesteen.com)

Printed and bound in China

THE GREAT VEGAN
GRAINS
BOOK

Celebrate Whole Grains with More Than
100 Delicious Plant-Based Recipes

CELINE STEEN & TAMASIN NOYES

FAIR WINDS

CONTENTS

THE WHOLE STORY ON WHOLE GRAINS

Grains have been a mainstay of the human diet throughout time and across cultures. As societies shifted toward a less nomadic lifestyle, they began to plant grains—from amaranth in Mexico, to barley in Egypt, to rye in Russia, to teff in Ethiopia, and so many more. Whole grains are believed to be some of the earliest cultivated foods, and they have been a vital component in sustaining life all around the world.

The popularity of whole grains is well deserved. Grains are delicious, highly nutritious, and packed with fiber, protein, and other key nutrients.

We all have increasingly busy lifestyles, and naturally this is reflected in the ways we cook. In this book, we have tried more than ever to offer you easy-to-prepare dishes that don't sacrifice flavor. Thanks to the diverse and delicious taste of whole grains, it's easy to use them as a backdrop for fresh vegetables, herbs, and spices, as well as in new and unique ways.

What follows is a list of questions (and answers!) to help you get started in exploring a diet richer in whole-grain, plant-based food.

WHAT MAKES A GRAIN A *WHOLE GRAIN*?

By definition, whole grains must retain their bran, germ, and endosperm in order to be deserving of the *whole grain* designation. The bran is the fiber-rich outer layer of the grain kernel. The germ is the nutrient- and protein-rich part of the grain. The endosperm is the germ's food supply and the largest part of the grain; it is carbohydrate rich and also provides a bit of protein.

There are some exceptions to this three-part rule, however. Some grains, such as barley and millet, need to have their inedible outer husks removed so that they're easier to digest. Such grains are still considered to be whole as they contain all the nutritional benefits found in the original kernel form.

Pearled and semipearled grains, on the other hand, cannot be considered whole. Although they offer the advantage of a much shorter cooking time, they are only slightly healthier for you than refined grains because the polishing process removes the bran (the outer layer) of the grain. Even more-refined grains, such as white rice, have the germ removed along with the bran, which definitely turns them into un-whole-y grains.

While we're clearly big fans of whole grains, we also think balance is key. Enjoy refined grains, on occasion, if the mood strikes!

WHY EAT WHOLE GRAINS?

Vegans probably eat more whole grains than you'd find in the average American diet. While that's a great start, the facts tell us that we should all find ways to get more whole grains in our diets. The health benefits speak for themselves.

Because a whole grain is truly whole, none of the natural nutritional benefits are removed. Whole grains are full of protein, fiber, B vitamins, antioxidants, and minerals. Do these sound familiar? They are some of the same nutritional elements that help reduce the risk of heart disease, type-2 diabetes, and even some types of cancer.

Whole grains also help to make us feel full and can help with weight control—we have fiber to thank for that. People who maintain a healthy weight tend to have better blood pressure and cholesterol levels. High levels of fiber are key to healthy digestion, too.

The 2010 USDA dietary guidelines say that half of our daily diet should be whole grains. Truly, we could go on and on about why whole grains should be a big part of your diet, but we think you get the idea.

STORING WHOLE GRAINS

To keep whole grains from going rancid or attracting bugs, it's best to store them in airtight containers such as glass or plastic jars, in a dry and cool place. It's helpful to add a sticky note to the package with the date of purchase. (Dating herbs and spices is also helpful to ensure you are using fresh-tasting, more potent ingredients for the best possible results.)

If you are new to whole grains and still experimenting with them, we recommend checking out bulk bins in order to get better acquainted with different grains. Bulk bins offer a wonderful opportunity to purchase smaller amounts. Plus, when you find one you love, you'll get a better price, too, as bulk grains are typically less expensive than the prepackaged versions.

PREPARING WHOLE GRAINS

Before you start cooking whole grains inspect them for debris, then rinse them in a fine-mesh sieve until the water runs clear. We don't always rinse tiny grains, (such as amaranth seeds and teff), but if you want to, line the sieve with a piece of cheesecloth or use a nut milk bag, instead, to avoid washing the grain down the drain.

Sprouting and soaking grains are popular techniques that are worthy of books devoted solely to them. If you'd like to get your feet—and your grains!—wet, we encourage you to check out the sidebar as well as online resources devoted to the topic.

For a nuttier flavor, you can toast rinsed, thoroughly drained, grains. Drizzle a little oil in a saucepan (the oil is optional, though the grain may stick otherwise). Add the grain, and cook it on medium-high heat for about 1 to 3 minutes, depending on the grain, or until the rinsing water has completely evaporated and the grain becomes fragrant and nutty.

Personally, we love our grains to remain al dente instead of mushy. Strangely enough, the instructions on most packages don't quite mesh with our textural preference. We recommend you adjust the amount of liquid and the cooking time according to the texture you prefer.

Cooking times can vary, depending on the freshness of the grains, as well as on the cooking tools that are used. The wisest thing to do is to keep an eye on grains as they are cooking. You can either drain the extra liquid once the desired texture is reached (like cooking pasta), or add more water or vegetable broth when the liquid is almost evaporated if the grain is still too al dente for your taste. Our favorite way to determine if a grain is cooked is to cut a few grains in half (if possible). The grain is ready if the color is uniform throughout and the grain is pleasingly chewy. One size definitely doesn't fit all in the whole-grains cooking world, but there's always room for adaptation!

To stop the cooking process once the grain has reached your preferred consistency, place the drained, cooked grain in an even layer on a large baking sheet. This allows it to cool more quickly than if it were left to cool in the sieve. Note that this step is not vital, but it is a good idea for people (like us) who are quite picky about texture.

For a detailed look at cooking methods and times for specific grains, please see the chart on pages 15–16.

TO SOAK OR NOT TO SOAK

Sometimes the instructions on the packaging suggest soaking the grains ahead of time. (We're looking at you, kamut!)

Soaking is used to shorten the cooking time, and it is also said to help unlock beneficial nutrients and make the grains more digestible. Raw plant-based foods contain antinutrients, such as enzyme inhibitors and phytic acid. These antinutrients prevent the body from absorbing all the minerals from the grains. Soaking makes it easier to receive optimal benefits from the grains we love to eat because it helps activate *phytase*, the enzyme responsible for breaking down phytic acid.

Opinions on the usefulness of soaking are quite divided. The decision to soak or not to soak is up to you. If you decide to soak, remember to check for doneness sooner than the chart (pages 15–16) indicates. Soaked grains may take a little less time to be ready.

As a general soaking rule, combine 1 tablespoon (15 ml) of an acidic agent, such as fresh lemon juice, enough filtered warm water to generously cover the grains and, of course, the whole grain itself. Place in a warm spot and soak overnight. While it's not vital to rinse the grains after soaking, we almost always do.

If we've planned ahead, soaking is our preferred method. If time is short, you can still get that grain cooked and on the table by using a quick-soak method. While this method doesn't break down the phytic acid like a longer soak does, it does reduce the cooking time and help obtain a better texture. To do a quick soak, bring a large pot of water to a boil, add the rinsed grain, and remove from the heat. Let soak for about 1 hour, then drain and cook according to the package directions. Just be sure to keep a close eye on the texture. Remember: Unless you're using a pressure cooker where you can't see the grain as it cooks, it's relatively difficult to overcook whole grains.

STORING *COOKED* WHOLE GRAINS

We love having cooked grains at the ready, especially when we're under a time crunch and don't feel like going for the quicker-cooking refined stuff. It's easy to eat well in a hurry if you cook some grain in advance, then cool and divide into portions before storing in the refrigerator or freezer. When properly stored in an airtight container in the refrigerator, cooked grains can last for a week. For freezer storage, simply place the portioned, cooked, and cooled grains in a large freezer bag, then lay flat and freeze on a baking sheet. This makes for easy storage once the grains are frozen because you can stack the bags. When a whole-grain craving hits, simply crack off a portion and let it thaw at room temperature or in the refrigerator. If you're even more pressed for time, you can run the freezer bag under warm water to defrost it.

GLUTEN-FREE GRAINS

Some of the whole grains included in this book are naturally gluten free—and proud of it! They are amaranth, black rice, buckwheat, corn, millet, oats, quinoa, brown rice (all types), sorghum, teff, and wild rice.

While these whole grains are naturally free of gluten, it's vital to remember that cross-contamination can happen. If you or the people for whom you are cooking are gluten sensitive, you absolutely *must* make sure to purchase whole grains that are certified gluten free and clearly labeled as such.

THE GRANARY

We keep lots of grains on hand at all times. They make meals hearty, satisfying, great-tasting, and—of course—healthy! If some of these grains and seeds aren't familiar to you, allow us to make the introductions. Be sure to see the cooking chart on pages 15–16. You'll be fast friends in no time.

Amaranth: Amaranth's tiny seeds were a major food source for the ancient Aztecs. Today, hummingbirds feed at the amaranth flowers, and we still enjoy the grain. These little gems are easy to cook and gluten free. Amaranth seeds are high in iron, calcium, and fiber. They are also high in lysine and methionine, which is unusual for a grain.

Barley: Just to be clear, it's *hulled* barley you're in the market for. Barley has been grown for 10,000 years, making it one of the oldest harvested grains. Historically, barley was popular in Tibet, and it was one of the first grains to be used in making fermented beverages. Best known today for its role in soups and stews, barley is fiber rich and is beneficial in maintaining blood-sugar levels.

Buckwheat: Hey, buckwheat, who are you trying to fool? You have nothing to do with wheat! You're even gluten free! Originally, buckwheat was grown in Southeast Asia; now the major producers are Russia and China. It has typically been used as flour, such as in buckwheat noodles. Like all grains, it is more healthful in its whole form. As a whole grain, buckwheat is called buckwheat groats until toasted, when it is then

WHAT ARE PSEUDOCEREALS?
Pseudocereals are actually seeds, botanically speaking, and not grains. Gluten-free pseudocereals include amaranth, buckwheat, millet, quinoa, and sorghum. They are commonly treated like grains in the culinary world, and they are included in the whole-grain category because they retain their bran, germ, and endosperm. The more, the merrier!

called kasha. Buckwheat is high in rutin and magnesium, both of which are instrumental in maintaining a healthy heart.

Bulgur: Bulgur is frequently mislabeled as cracked wheat. Technically speaking, bulgur really *is* cracked wheat. More accurately, it is made from raw wheat berries that are parboiled, then hulled, dried, and finally cracked. On the other hand, cracked wheat is just, well, cracked. Bulgur comes in various grinds, and it is even available in a form that solely requires soaking in hot liquid (in true couscous-like fashion). This cookbook does *not* call for soaking-only bulgur. We use Bob's Red Mill Quick-Cooking Bulgur.

Cracked wheat: Bulgur? Cracked wheat? Which is it? While they're often used interchangeably, they're not one and the same. Cracked wheat is as straightforward as it sounds: It is made from raw wheat berries that are carefully milled to obtain smaller, quicker-cooking pieces of wheat. While the cooking time is reduced, rest assured that the berries do not lose any nutritional value during this process.

Einkorn: One of the lesser-known forms of wheat, this grain has become one of our favorites. It holds the distinction of being the only form of wheat that has never been hybridized. It's truly an ancient grain: Einkorn farms circa 7500 BCE have been unearthed in Turkey. In Morocco, France, and other countries, einkorn is typically grown as animal feed. While we love animals, they're not keeping this one to themselves! The grain is high in protein, B vitamins, and iron. It is also versatile and tastes incredible. Special note: Some people with wheat sensitivity have found einkorn to be less of a trigger. We aren't advocating einkorn for gluten-free people, but if you want to try it, do so with caution.

Farro, also known as emmer: Even though emmer is an old kid on the block and was already around in the Middle East centuries ago, its popularity waned because of the more laid back (as in, quicker to hull) durum wheat grain. We're happy to report emmer is finally getting over being snubbed and making quite a comeback these days, especially in Italy, with its now world-famous name *farro* or *farro medio*.

Freekeh: Originally from the Middle East, freekeh has been gaining in popularity. It is available in both a cracked form and a whole form. They can be used interchangeably in many recipes, just be sure to adjust the cooking time. Technically, freekeh is young, green wheat. It's high in fiber, protein, and trace minerals such as iron and zinc. Like most grains, it's also incredibly versatile.

Kamut: It's news to us (and probably to you) that Kamut is actually a brand name for khorasan wheat. Its roots—yes, we went there—are usually (and incorrectly) believed to be Egyptian. It's true that the grain was rediscovered in 1949 and that it is protein rich and packed with minerals. Interestingly, kamut is lower in fiber but higher in fatty acids than other grains, making it an energy booster. Plus, "kamut" is just fun to say.

Millet: It turns out that millet, the small, gluten-free, pale-colored seed most of us are best acquainted with, is the name of a whole group of related grains that have been used for thousands of years. For example, teff (page 13) is also part of the millet family. For clarity's sake, the millet we call for is the most readily available type of millet on the market. We find it benefits from being toasted before cooking to boost the naturally nutty, almost cornlike flavor. Toasting also enhances millet's ability to absorb cooking liquids. We highly recommend spending a few additional minutes to toast millet because the cooking time of this protein-rich grain is fairly short.

Oats: Oats, we've loved you since way back when. We loved you before we knew how good you are for us. Okay, not as far back as when you were first found growing wild in the Near East. More like since you were domesticated in Europe around 600 BCE. Or almost. We've got as many reasons as oats have grinds. Oats rival soy in terms of protein content, are full of fiber, and are known to reduce cholesterol. We've used oat groats and steel-cut oats in this book. Oat groats are made from hulled, whole oats; steel-cut oats are oat groats that have been cut into smaller pieces.

Polenta and corn grits: Before the 1600s, polenta was made from a number of different grains—and even chickpeas. Polenta goes by many names and comes in many forms (now all corn based). Perhaps the oldest name used in America would be maize. Grits (a coarse grind) are more common in the southern United States. Corn grits are treated with niacin, a form of alkali that is missing from the grain. All forms are high in protein, fiber, iron, zinc, and more. Look for brands (such as Bob's Red Mill) that use the whole corn kernel without removing the bran and germ.

Quinoa: Quinoa hardly needs an introduction because its reputation as a superfood precedes it. Nope, superfood is not a real food term, but it gets the point across. Quinoa was first cultivated in South America back in the BCE days. In fact, the Incas considered it a sacred food. Quinoa is high in protein, essential amino acids, and more. It's a good source of calcium, too, which is a big win for vegans . . . and everyone else!

Rice: Ah . . . rice . . . your backstory is a bit harder to get our heads around. We'll admit to growing up on plain old white rice. Now exciting, colorful varieties seem to be multiplying on our grocery shelves. The purple, red, and even brown varieties have more antioxidants and a higher fiber content than white. All these cool new types of rice can trace their lineage to China—for those who are keeping track, that part is certain. In this book, we've used black rice, wild rice, and several kinds of brown rice (such as short-grain brown rice, sweet brown rice, and jasmine brown rice).

Rye: When we think of rye, we automatically jump to Eastern and Central Europe—and to Reuben sandwiches. You'll find no Reubens in this book: Here, it's straight up whole rye berries! Rye is closely related to both barley and wheat, yet recent studies have shown it to be far more filling than equal amounts of wheat. Like all grains, rye is high in fiber and is also healthful for the heart and cholesterol levels.

Sorghum, also known as milo: It has been suggested that this gluten-free grain has its origins in Africa thousands of years ago. Despite its respectable age, sorghum hasn't yet reached the same level of fame and popularity as quinoa in the U.S. and Europe. Indeed, about half of the sorghum production is destined to become animal feed. It's time to give sorghum a chance in our everyday cooking! Sorghum is great in salads and pilafs. It is sturdy enough to hold its shape and texture in soups and stews, too. We fondly refer to it as millet's heftier cousin, but feel it's the most finicky grain to cook out of the bunch. Sorghum should *not* be left with a toothsome bite (like kamut, for example), but must be fully tender (like rice) to be enjoyed. A quick soak or overnight soak is mandatory with this grain. Surprisingly, sorghum's cooking time does not change with the soak: It still needs approximately 1 hour to reach proper tenderness. We also find that cooked sorghum tends to get almost unpleasantly chewy when chilled. It is at its best when eaten at its freshest—still warm, or reheated, or at room temperature.

Spelt, or *farro grande*: The history of spelt is a little sketchy, but its popularity grew fast. Spelt appears to have popped up simultaneously on two different continents (Europe and Asia), leaving scientists to wonder just who its plant parents are. We do know that it hit the United States around the 1890s. However, the U.S. switched most early spelt fields over to grow varieties of hard wheat used in bread baking. Nowadays, organic farms are bringing spelt back to the mainstream. Spelt is high in fiber, protein, vitamins, and minerals.

Teff: Tiny—but mighty—teff grains are actually part of the millet family. One of the most important food sources of Ethiopia, teff is mostly known elsewhere as the main ingredient of Ethiopian injera flatbread. It is slowly finding some well-deserved popularity as the world realizes teff is also great to use in porridge, soups, and even salads when cooked into a more pilaflike state (simply use a lower liquid-to-grain ratio). We also love it for its high calcium content, the highest of any grain, with 123 mg per cooked cup (252 g).

SWAPPING GRAINS

Are the grains interchangeable in this book? Yes! Many of them are, and we've made sure to add notes to the recipes where it applies so that you can choose what you want, depending on availability, cost, and personal preference. In general, grains with similar textures (e.g., einkorn for barley, or spelt for kamut) can be swapped. Note that if such changes are made, it is likely that cooking times will be different as well. Always refer to the basic instructions on the package, our grain chart, (pages 15–16), or to your own knowledge of the grain.

Triticale berries: Triticale berries are the love child—or more scientifically speaking, the hybridized result—of the wheat and rye union. This relatively young grain fell out of favor shortly after appearing on the market approximately forty years ago. Thankfully, it is experiencing a successful comeback as its sturdiness makes it a great candidate for organic and sustainable farming.

Whole wheat kernels: Whole wheat comes in many forms: einkorn, farro, kamut, spelt, red or white wheat berries, spring or winter wheat berries, hard or soft wheat berries, as well as bulgur and cracked wheat for quicker-cooking results. There's clearly no lack of choice in the wheat family! Some of these grains are predominantly milled into flour for baked goods or pasta, and wheat is the uncontested leader of whole grains that contain gluten (a protein composite that makes for stretchy bread dough). Wheat is also un-doubtedly revered in its most unprocessed form: whole (or cracked) and cooked.

THE GRAIN CHART

To make the grain-cooking process a breeze, refer to the cooking chart and instructions that follow. Keep in mind that the information in the chart is to be used as a general guideline. There may be variations in the amount of liquid needed, the cooking time, and the yield, depending on the grain itself.

The Absorption Method

For all grains: If you prefer, soak (page 9) or toast (page 8) the grain in advance. Place the picked-through, rinsed, drained grain in a large saucepan to allow for a more even cooking process. Add the cooking liquid (water, or water with Broth Powder [page 167], or vegetable broth, or pineapple juice [page 22]).

Bring to a boil, fully or loosely cover (follow recipe instructions), and simmer as needed. Note that the cooking time in the chart refers to when the grain is set to sim-mer. Check occasionally to make sure the grain reaches your preferred texture. Drain or add extra liquid, if needed.

Pasta Style

An alternative method is to cook the grain pasta style by placing it in a large saucepan, covering it with about 2 to 3 inches (5 to 7.5 cm) of cooking liquid, bringing to a boil, and loosely covering while cooking on medium-low heat until the desired texture is reached. Once ready, drain the extra liquid. This method wastes slightly more liquid than the absorption method, but we find it yields a better texture in many cases. The choice is entirely up to you.

DRY GRAIN	COOKING LIQUID	COOKING TIME (or until preferred texture is reached, check sooner if soaked)	APPROXIMATE YIELD
Amaranth 1 cup (180 g)	2 cups (470 ml)	15 to 20 min.	2½ cups (615 g)
Barley, Hulled 1 cup (184 g)	3 cups (705 ml)	30 to 40 min.	3 cups (472 g)
Black Rice 1 cup (180 g)	2 cups (470 ml)	25 min.	2 cups (345 g)
Brown Rice, Long Grain 1 cup (185 g)	1¾ cups (415 ml)	30 to 40 min.	3 cups (585 g)
Brown Rice, Medium Grain 1 cup (190 g)	2½ cups (590 ml)	45 to 55 min.	3 cups (585 g)
Brown Rice, Sweet 1 cup (196 g)	2 cups (470 ml)	35 to 45 min.	3 cups (480 g)
Buckwheat Groats 1 cup (180 g)	2 cups (470 ml)	10 min.	2½ cups (420 g)
Bulgur, Quick Cooking 1 cup (160 g)	2 cups (470 ml)	12 to 15 min. (plus left to stand 10 min, fluff)	3 cups (500 g)
Cracked Wheat 1 cup (160 g)	2 cups (470 ml)	15 min. (plus left to stand 10 min, fluff)	3 cups (500 g)
Einkorn 1 cup (192 g)	3 cups (705 ml)	30 to 35 min.	3 cups (454 g)
Farro 1 cup (208 g)	2½ cups (590 ml)	20 to 30 min.	2 cups (330 g)
Freekeh, Cracked 1 cup (184 g)	2½ cups (590 ml)	20 min.	2¼ cups (520 g)
Freekeh, Whole 1 cup (160 g)	2½ cups (590 ml)	40 min.	2½ cups (420 g)
Kamut 1 cup (184 g)	3 cups (705 ml)	Overnight soak, 45 to 60 min.	3 cups (516 g)
Millet 1 cup (220 g)	2 cups (470 ml)	15 to 20 min.	2½ cups (435 g)
Oats, Groats 1 cup (184 g)	3 cups (705 ml)	30 min. for pilaflike results.	2 cups (305 g)
Oats, Steel Cut 1 cup (176 g)	3 cups (705 ml)	10 min. for al dente, 20 min. for creamy	2⅔ cups (650 g)
Polenta and Corn Grits 1 cup (140 g)	3 cups (705 ml)	5 to 10 min. (plus let stand 5 minutes)	2⅔ cups (714 g)
Quinoa 1 cup (170 g)	2 cups (470 ml)	12 to 15 min. (plus left to stand 10 min, fluff)	3 cups (555 g)

(continued) >

DRY GRAIN	COOKING LIQUID	COOKING TIME (or until preferred texture is reached, check sooner if soaked)	APPROXIMATE YIELD
Rye Berries 1 cup (180 g)	3½ cups (825 ml)	Overnight soak, 45 to 60 min.	3 cups (425 g)
Sorghum 1 cup (204 g)	4 cups (940 ml)	Overnight soak, 60 min.	3 cups (496 g)
Spelt Berries 1 cup (180 g)	3½ cups (825 ml)	Overnight soak, 45 to 60 min.	3 cups (583 g)
Teff 1 cup (200 g)	2 to 3 cups (470 to 705 ml) (see recipes)	10 to 20 min. (see recipes)	2½ cups (630 g)
Triticale Berries 1 cup (180 g)	3½ cups (825 ml)	Overnight soak, 45 to 60 min.	2½ cups (410 g)
Wheat Berries, Soft White 1 cup (192 g)	3½ cups (825 ml)	Overnight soak, 45 to 60 min.	2½ cups (400 g)
Wild Rice 1 cup (160 g)	3 cups (705 ml)	45 to 50 min.	3½ cups (574 g)

GLOSSARY

We strive to use readily available ingredients in all our recipes. If you cannot locate some of the following ingredients at your local grocery store, international foods store, or natural food store, don't forget to check online! Whenever available and affordable, choose organic ingredients over conventional ones.

Berbere spice: Berbere is an Ethiopian spice mix made with fenugreek, chile, and paprika. It has varying levels of heat, depending on the brand (such as Frontier). It's best to use it to taste. Berbere can be purchased at well-stocked markets and online or can be home-made. There's a good recipe on www.epicurious.com, originally from Gourmet. Just search for "Ethiopian Spice Mix (Berbere)."

Black salt (a.k.a. *kala namak*): This salt is actually not black but rose pink, and it should not be confused with black lava salt. Kala namak imparts an egglike flavor to foods because of the sulfur it contains.

Chana dal: These dried, split baby chickpeas are a great source of protein and fiber. They are also a tasty, slightly larger alternative to lentils. We love pairing them up with vegetables and whole grains in Chana Dal Dalia (page 72) and Moroccan Wheat Berries (page 63). Chana dal can be purchased at international food stores and online.

Chickpea flour: Also known as gram flour, garbanzo bean flour, and besan, this protein-rich flour is made from ground chickpeas. It is quite bitter when eaten in raw form, so do not have a taste of any uncooked. Garbanzo fava bean flour (a blend of chickpea and fava bean flours) can be used instead of chickpea flour.

Fire-roasted tomatoes: These are used in a few of our dishes, but we know they can be hard to find. Tester and friend Liz Wyman replaces them with regular diced tomatoes and adds a few drops of liquid smoke to make up for the lack of roasted flavor.

Harissa spice: This spicy North African flavoring is made from a blend of hot peppers and other spices. It comes in a paste or dry blend: You can use either form in equal amounts, to taste. Harissa can be found in the ethnic aisle of well-stocked grocery stores or online.

Miso: This fermented soybean paste has many uses and it comes in several flavors and sharpness levels. The kind we use the most is mellow white miso (also known as shiro miso), preferably organic. Miso can be found in most Asian grocery stores and in the refrigerated section of your local health food store.

Neutral-flavored oils: Neutral-flavored oils don't overwhelm the other flavors of the dishes in which they're used. Our favorite neutral-flavored oils include corn oil, grape-seed oil, light olive oil, peanut oil, safflower oil, and more.

Nutritional yeast: This flaky, flavorful, yellow yeast is usually grown on molasses. It has an umami-rich, kind of cheesy taste, and it adds a B-vitamin boost to foods if you use formulas labeled as "vegetarian support." It can be found in the vitamin and supplement section of most health food stores. The flakes vary in size, which makes for a weight that also varies. We buy ours in bulk (it's less expensive that way), and the flakes look quite fine. If you can only find large flakes, pulse them in a food processor a couple of times before measuring in order to get the most accurate results.

Salt: For the most part, we prefer telling you to use salt "to taste" instead of giving a set amount. Just remember, it's easier to add extra salt than it is to remove it! We use both coarse kosher salt and fine sea salt. If you don't have coarse kosher salt, use half the amount of fine sea salt wherever kosher salt is called for.

Sriracha: Sriracha is a hot chili sauce from Thailand. New versions are popping up all the time. Just be sure to check ingredients as some brands include fish paste.

Tamari: Tamari is a richly flavored, Japanese-style soy sauce. We prefer gluten-free reduced-sodium tamari. If you cannot find tamari, use reduced-sodium soy sauce in its place. (The Gluten-Free Potential icon won't apply anymore if gluten-free tamari is replaced with soy sauce.)

Vegan bouillon: We opt for a bouillon paste made by Superior Touch when available. Look for the No Chicken and No Beef versions of Better than Bouillon in the soup aisle. If cubes are more readily available, substitute one crumbled cube per teaspoon of paste. We like the Edward & Sons bouillon cubes. (At the time of writing, Better than Bouillon No Beef contains soy. If soy is a concern for you, double check the labels.)

Vegan milks: Two of our favorites are the unsweetened, plain, almond milk and the almond-coconut blend. You can use whatever you prefer, just remember to go with unsweetened plain vegan milk for savory applications.

Whole-wheat pastry flour: If this flour isn't available, you can also use an equal combination of whole-wheat flour and all-purpose flour, or only all-purpose flour instead (1:1 ratio).

RECIPE ICONS

Many of the recipes contained in this cookbook are labeled with one or more of the following icons:

▶ GLUTEN-FREE POTENTIAL

Recipes that can be safe to enjoy by those who need to eat gluten-free foods. Make sure to thoroughly check ingredients for safe use and purchase ingredients that are certified gluten-free. Contact the manufacturer, if needed, for up-to-date information.

▶ SOY-FREE POTENTIAL

Recipes that are free of any soy products, provided soymilk isn't used wherever vegan milk is called for. Please thoroughly check labels and contact the manufacturer, if needed. Be sure to check unexpected ingredients such as vegetable broth and nut milks as they may contain hidden soy. If using nonstick cooking spray, remember to check for soy lecithin, too. If you cannot find soy-free nonstick cooking spray, use an oil spray instead.

▶ QUICK AND EASY

Recipes that take fewer than 30 minutes to whip up, provided you have intermediate cooking or baking skills. (If the grains are cooked ahead of time, the preparation of many of our recipes takes mere minutes.)

EYE-OPENING GRAINS

Getting Up on the Grain Side of the Bed

We all know how important breakfast is, and how healthy whole grains are, so why not start your day by getting up on the grain side of the bed? Whether you prefer sweet or savory first thing in the morning, you'll find our recipes are tasty, energizing, and filling. They will also power you through busy mornings. This chapter will get you started, and the following chapters are yours for the feasting throughout the day.

Breakfast Barley

▶ **GRAIN**: BARLEY ▶ SOY-FREE POTENTIAL

Just the aroma of this one will wake up your taste buds. All it takes is the first bite to know you'll be good to go until lunch!

½ cup (92 g) dry hulled barley, rinsed and drained

1 cup (235 ml) water

¼ cup (60 ml) apple cider

¼ cup (60 ml) orange juice

¼ cup (25 g) fresh cranberries, roughly chopped in half

1 tablespoon (9 g) raisins, optional

1 tablespoon (20 g) pure maple syrup

½ teaspoon ground cinnamon

Pinch fine sea salt

Combine all the ingredients in a small saucepan. Bring to a boil, then cover the saucepan. Reduce the heat to simmer. Cook, stirring occasionally, until the barley is tender and the liquid is absorbed, about 50 minutes. If extra liquid remains, remove the cover and let cook a few minutes longer until the barley has absorbed the liquid. Serve hot.

YIELD: 2 servings

Apple Butter Spiced Millet

▶ **GRAIN:** MILLET ▶ SOY-FREE POTENTIAL ▶ GLUTEN-FREE POTENTIAL

In order to put a well-deserved spotlight on millet, the poor, underrated gluten-free whole grain, we've come up with a scrumptious sweet breakfast bowl. It's guaranteed to help shoo the morning blues away with a welcomed warmth, richness, and creaminess.

1 cup (235 ml) full-fat canned coconut milk

1¾ cups (415 ml) water, more if needed

¼ cup plus 2 tablespoons (90 g) unsweetened apple butter

½ teaspoon ground cinnamon

¼ teaspoon ground ginger

⅛ teaspoon ground nutmeg

⅛ teaspoon ground allspice

Pinch fine sea salt

½ cup (110 g) dry millet, ground into farina (see Recipe Notes)

3 tablespoons to ¼ cup (60 to 80 g) pure maple syrup, to taste

1 teaspoon pure vanilla extract

¼ cup (30 g) toasted pecan bits and pieces

Place the milk, water, apple butter, cinnamon, ginger, nutmeg, allspice, and salt in a medium saucepan. Bring to a low boil on medium-high heat. Lower the heat and slowly whisk in the millet farina, stirring to avoid lumps.

Cover partially with a lid and simmer until thickened but still creamy, about 20 minutes, stirring occasionally. Add extra water as needed to reach desired tenderness, and extend the cooking time if needed. Remove from the heat. Stir the syrup and vanilla into the millet. Let stand 5 minutes before serving. Divide among 4 bowls, and top each serving with pecans.

YIELD: 4 servings

Recipe Notes

- Make your bowl of warm millet pumpkin-y by replacing the apple butter with the same amount of pure canned pumpkin (not pie mix) or pumpkin butter.

- For prettier and even tastier results, prepare a batch of roasted pears or apples (page 24) to top each serving.

- Farina consistency is obtained by grinding the grains into a fine yet granular consistency, similar to ground nuts. A coffee grinder or small blender works well. Grind the millet in 2 to 3 batches for best results.

Quinoa Breakfast Pilaf

▶ GRAIN: QUINOA ▶ SOY-FREE POTENTIAL ▶ GLUTEN-FREE POTENTIAL

This simple recipe lets the flavors of its ingredients shine, creating a meal that's beautiful to look at and good for you as well.

1 cup (235 ml) water

1 cup (235 ml) unsweetened pineapple juice, plus more for serving

1 cup (170 g) dry ivory quinoa, rinsed and drained

2 tablespoons (30 ml) pure lemon juice

1 cup (150 g) pomegranate seeds (see Recipe Notes)

Orange zest, to taste and optional

2 tablespoons (11 g) minced fresh mint, optional

1 cup (140 g) dry roasted whole cashews, coarsely chopped (see Recipe Notes)

½ cup (30 g) toasted unsweetened coconut flakes (see Recipe Notes)

In a saucepan fitted with a lid, bring the water and pineapple juice to a boil. Add the quinoa, lower the heat, and simmer covered until the liquid is absorbed and the quinoa is tender, about 15 to 20 minutes. Let stand 5 minutes. Fluff with a fork, and set aside to cool to room temperature.

In a medium bowl, gently fold the lemon juice, pomegranate seeds, and zest into the quinoa. Divide into 4 portions, and top each portion with 1½ teaspoons mint, ¼ cup (35 g) cashews, 2 tablespoons (8 g) coconut flakes, and a drizzle of (warm or cold) pineapple juice. Serve immediately.

YIELD: 4 servings

Recipe Notes

- For extra sweetness, add 1 tablespoon or more (20 g or more) pure maple syrup or agave nectar to the grains once cooked.

- For extra creaminess, stir a little vegan yogurt (plain or vanilla, unsweetened or not) in the pilaf.

- To toast coconut flakes, preheat the oven to 325°F (170°C, or gas mark 3). Place the flakes on a baking sheet. Bake until golden brown and fragrant, stirring occasionally to prevent burning, about 10 minutes total. Set aside to cool.

- To roast cashews, preheat the oven to 325°F (170°C, or gas mark 3). Place the cashews on a baking sheet. Bake until golden brown and fragrant, stirring occasionally to prevent burning, about 15 minutes total. Set aside to cool.

- You can replace some or all of the pomegranate seeds with cubed fresh pineapple, mango, or chopped slices of orange.

- We love to eat this with other grains as well by combining half of the quinoa with 1 cup (174 g) cooked millet (as shown in photo at right).

Roasted Pear Buckwheat Porridge

▶ **GRAIN**: BUCKWHEAT ▶ SOY-FREE POTENTIAL ▶ GLUTEN-FREE POTENTIAL

This porridge recipe converted us into big buckwheat-for-breakfast fans. We recommend you double the roasted pear ingredients if you want to use the cubes from the two extra pears as garnish—they're that delicious and pretty. If you aren't a fan of pears, replace them with apples.

½ cup (90 g) dry buckwheat groats

1 cup (235 ml) filtered water

1½ tablespoons (23 ml) fresh lemon juice, divided

Nonstick cooking spray or oil spray

2 teaspoons (4 g) packed grated peeled fresh ginger

1 tablespoon (20 g) pure maple syrup or agave nectar, plus extra for serving

2 firm Bartlett pears (about 12 ounces, or 340 g), cored, cut into ½-inch (1.3 cm) cubes

¼ cup plus 2 tablespoons (90 ml) unsweetened plain almond milk

2 tablespoons (32 g) natural toasted hazelnut butter, cashew butter, or almond butter

2 teaspoons (10 ml) pure vanilla extract

¼ teaspoon ground cinnamon

In a medium glass measuring cup, combine the groats with the water and 1½ teaspoons lemon juice. Cover and soak for 8 hours at room temperature.

Preheat the oven to 400°F (200°C, or gas mark 6). Lightly coat a 9-inch (23 cm) baking pan with cooking spray. Combine the remaining 1 tablespoon (15 ml) lemon juice, ginger, and maple syrup in a medium bowl. Add the pear cubes and gently toss to coat. Spread in an even layer in the prepared pan. Roast until tender and slightly golden, turning the pears once halfway through, about 20 to 25 minutes. Set aside and let cool. (This can be done the night before. Store the pears in an airtight container in the refrigerator if preparing in advance.)

Drain the soaking water, rinsing the groats thoroughly (the groats might be slightly slimy, but it doesn't affect the outcome). Transfer to a food processor or blender along with the roasted pears, milk, hazelnut butter, vanilla, and cinnamon. Process until mostly smooth. Serve immediately with a drizzle of maple syrup if desired, or store in an airtight container in the refrigerator until chilled or for up to 2 days. The porridge can be gently reheated if you prefer eating something warm for breakfast.

YIELD: 2 servings

Teff and Amaranth Porridge

▶ **GRAINS**: TEFF AND AMARANTH ▶ SOY-FREE POTENTIAL ▶ QUICK AND EASY
▶ GLUTEN-FREE POTENTIAL

Enjoy this healthy, yet decadent-tasting, porridge as is, or topped with toasted nuts or fresh fruit. Try toasted cashews with fresh pineapple or mango cubes, or toasted walnuts with sliced ripe persimmons or yellow kiwi. You can make this recipe with teff alone if you'd like, but we don't recommend using only amaranth as the flavor can be a little overwhelming on its own.

¼ cup (50 g) dry teff

¼ cup (45 g) dry amaranth
(or same amount of dry teff)

1 cup (235 ml) water

1 cup (235 ml) canned coconut milk
(or other vegan milk, for lighter results)

3 tablespoons (30 g) golden raisins

¼ teaspoon ground cinnamon, ginger,
or cardamom

1 to 2 tablespoons (20 to 40 g) agave
nectar or pure maple syrup, to taste

Fresh fruit of choice, cubed or sliced
if needed

Optional: chopped toasted nuts or
toasted coconut flakes (page 22)
for garnish

Place the teff, amaranth, and water in a small saucepan. Bring to a gentle boil, lower the heat. Cover with a lid and simmer until the water is absorbed, about 10 minutes. Add extra water if you want a softer porridge. Remove from the heat, leave covered, and let stand 5 minutes.

Add the coconut milk and raisins. Continue simmering until thickened to a porridge-like consistency, about 8 minutes. Stir the cinnamon to combine and add agave to taste. We love this porridge when it's slightly chilled for 30 minutes to 1 hour, but our testers enjoyed it warm as well. Divide in breakfast bowls. Top with fruit of choice, if desired, and nuts or coconut flakes.

YIELD: 2 large or 4 small servings

Apricot Oats

▶ **GRAIN**: STEEL-CUT OATS ▶ GLUTEN-FREE POTENTIAL ▶ SOY-FREE POTENTIAL
▶ QUICK AND EASY

This sweet start to any day can also be served as a comforting dinner. With a double dose of apricots, this healthy porridge tastes more like a gourmet cookie. Go ahead, indulge yourself!

½ cup (88 g) steel-cut oats

1½ cups (355 ml) water

4 dried apricot halves, chopped

2 tablespoons (38 g) apricot jam

¼ teaspoon ground cinnamon

Pinch fine sea salt

Pure maple syrup, for serving

Combine the oats, water, apricots, jam, cinnamon, and salt in a small saucepan over medium heat. Bring to a boil, reduce to a simmer, and cover. Cook, stirring occasionally, for 20 to 25 minutes. The oats will be tender and the liquid should be absorbed. If not, remove the lid and cook a few minutes longer. Serve with maple syrup on the side.

YIELD: 2 servings

Blueberry Polenta Triangles

▶ **GRAIN**: POLENTA ▶ GLUTEN-FREE POTENTIAL ▶ SOY-FREE POTENTIAL

Tami grew up eating mush for breakfast, so coming up with polenta breakfast recipes felt as if she was coming home. Citrus always plays so well with blueberries, as does the corn. Fry them up for a quick morning treat.

¾ cup (180 ml) orange juice

¾ cup (180 ml) water

½ cup (70 g) polenta

1 tablespoon (13 g) evaporated cane juice

Pinch fine sea salt

½ cup (75 g) blueberries

Neutral-flavored oil, for cooking

Pure maple syrup, for serving

Vegan butter, for serving

Line a loaf pan with parchment paper, being sure to reach about 2 inches (5 cm) up the sides.

Bring the orange juice and water to a boil in a medium-size saucepan over high heat. Whisk in the polenta, evaporated cane juice, and salt. Reduce the heat to simmer. Continue whisking for 5 to 10 minutes until the mixture is thick and clears the bottom of the pan. Remove from the heat and gently stir in the blueberries. Pour into the prepared loaf pan and let cool for 30 minutes. You want a flat plank of polenta in a loaf-pan shape. Refrigerate for a minimum of 2 hours until the polenta is very firm. At this stage, if wrapped airtight and refrigerated, the polenta can be stored for up to 1 week.

To cook the polenta, lift the parchment paper carefully from the loaf pan. Cut the polenta in half, and then cut each half again to create 4 triangles. Pour a ¼-inch (6 mm) layer of oil in a large skillet and heat over medium heat. Add the triangles. Do not move them until the bottom is slightly browned, about 4 to 6 minutes. Moving them too soon can remove the crisp outer coating. Turn over the triangles and cook the second side until browned and crisp, about 4 to 6 minutes. Serve hot.

YIELD: 4 triangles

Mom's Polenta

To make Mom's polenta, use 1½ cups (355 ml) water, ½ cup (70 g) polenta, and a pinch of salt. Follow the recipe directions as written on page 37.

Apples and Oats French Toast

▶ **GRAIN:** STEEL-CUT OATS ▶ SOY-FREE POTENTIAL ▶ QUICK AND EASY

Gently spiced apples are the perfect match for the crunchy, only slightly sweet French toast. The very best version of this we've ever had was from apples we'd picked ourselves. It's an ideal way to start your day or wrap it up with a homey dinner.

FOR THE APPLES:

2 teaspoons (10 g) vegan butter or oil

2 McIntosh (or favorite) apples, peeled, cored, and diced

¼ teaspoon ground cinnamon

Pinch fine sea salt

2 tablespoons (40 g) pure maple syrup, plus more for serving

FOR THE FRENCH TOAST:

1 cup (176 g) steel-cut oats

1½ cups (180 g) all-purpose flour

¼ cup (52 g) evaporated cane juice

2 teaspoons (9 g) baking powder

¾ teaspoon ground cinnamon

Pinch fine sea salt

1¼ cups (295 ml) plain, unsweetened vegan milk, more if needed

1 teaspoon pure vanilla extract or maple extract

12 slices (1-inch, or 2.5 cm) stale French bread

High heat neutral-flavored oil, for cooking

To make the apples: Melt the butter in a medium-size skillet over medium heat. Add the apples, cinnamon, and salt. Cook, stirring occasionally, for 3 to 5 minutes until the apples have softened. Add the maple syrup and stir to coat the apples. Cook for 1 to 2 minutes to heat through, and then set aside. If necessary, reheat the apples over low heat when serving.

To make the French toast: Put the oats in a blender. Briefly process the oats until they are no longer whole, but do not grind into flour. Pour the oats into a baking dish. Add the flour, sugar, baking powder, cinnamon, and salt. Stir with a fork to combine. Stir in the milk and vanilla so that all the dry ingredients are wet. The mixture will be thick, but some lumps are okay.

Heat a thin layer of oil in a large skillet over medium to medium-high heat. Dip both sides of the bread into the batter, then put the bread into the hot oil. The mixture tends to thicken as it sits, so add splashes of milk as needed. Cook for 3 to 5 minutes until golden. Turn over to cook the second side for 2 to 4 minutes or until golden. Cook the remaining slices in the same way.

To serve, put 3 slices of French toast on a plate and top with one-quarter of the apples. Drizzle with the additional maple syrup.

YIELD: 4 servings

Sausage Smash Potato Hash

▶ **GRAIN**: CRACKED FREEKEH

We've taken the ever-popular scramble idea and made it even better by creating a one-dish potato, sausage, and tofu (or bean) masterpiece. Serve it with a side of fruit and start your day with a smile.

8 ounces (227 g) golden potatoes, cut into ½-inch (1.3 cm) pieces

1 to 2 tablespoons (15 to 30 ml) high heat neutral-flavored oil

8 ounces (227 g) extra-firm tofu, pressed and crumbled, or 1 cup (256 g) cooked cannellini beans

½ onion, chopped

½ bell pepper, chopped (any color)

½ recipe Sausage Crumbles (page 34) (not cooked)

2 cloves garlic, minced

2 tablespoons (15 g) nutritional yeast

2 tablespoons (30 ml) dry white wine, or broth

1 tablespoon (15 ml) tamari

2 tablespoons (30 ml) vegetable broth

Salt and pepper

Hot sauce, optional

Put the chopped potatoes in a medium-size pot. Cover with water and a generous pinch of salt. Bring to a boil, reduce to a simmer, and cook for 12 to 14 minutes until tender. Drain and refrigerate for 2 hours or longer for the best texture.

Heat 1 tablespoon (15 ml) of the oil in a large skillet over medium heat. Add the potatoes, tofu (if using), onion, and bell pepper. Cook, stirring occasionally, for 5 to 7 minutes until the vegetables are tender. Add the additional oil if the mixture is sticking. Add the beans (if using), the Sausage Crumble mixture, and the garlic. Cook for 3 to 4 minutes to heat throughout. Add the nutritional yeast, wine, and tamari, scraping any bits off the bottom of the skillet. Cook for 3 to 5 minutes for the flavors to meld, adding splashes of broth as needed to prevent sticking. Season to taste with salt and pepper. Serve with the hot sauce on the side.

YIELD: 2 servings

Recipe Note

Are you a munch-on-the-run type? Stuff this hash in a burrito and wrap it in foil to enjoy any time.

Sausage Crumbles

▶ **GRAIN:** CRACKED FREEKEH ▶ SOY-FREE POTENTIAL

These savory sausage crumbles are easy to make and the ideal side to any breakfast main dish. For a kick to really wake you up, add the cayenne pepper. If you prefer to ease your palate into the day, feel free to leave it out.

1¼ cups (295 ml) water

½ cup (92 g) cracked freekeh

1 tablespoon (7 g) ground flaxseed

Generous pinch fine sea salt

1 tablespoon (15 g) organic ketchup

2 teaspoons (5 g) onion powder

1 teaspoon paprika

¼ to ½ teaspoon ground fennel seeds

½ teaspoon garlic powder

½ teaspoon rubbed sage

½ teaspoon ground black pepper

½ teaspoon pure maple syrup

¼ teaspoon dried thyme

¼ teaspoon ground cayenne, or more to taste, optional

Nonstick cooking spray, for cooking

High heat neutral-flavored oil, for cooking

Combine the water, freekeh, flaxseed, and salt in a small saucepan. Bring to a boil and reduce the heat to simmer. Cook for 20 to 25 minutes, stirring frequently, until the mixture is very thick. The mixture should be so thick that it easily stays on one side of the pot when stirred to that side. Remove from the heat and stir in the remaining ingredients.

Heat a thin layer of oil in a large skillet over medium heat. Crumble the sausage mixture into the skillet. Cook the sausage crumbles until browned, stirring occasionally, for 10 to 14 minutes.

YIELD: 8 servings

GRAIN MAINS FOR ALL APPETITES

Filling Your Plate with Whole Grain Goodness

It's high time whole grains took their proper place on the plate! For far too long, they were viewed as just a way to round out a meal—but no more. We've packed this chapter with recipes that place grains front and center, and they are sure to hit the spot whether it's as a light lunch or hearty dinner. With lots of international influences, as well as some American leanings, these recipes will satisfy cravings you might not even realize you have.

Spelt and Bean Burritos

▶ **GRAIN:** SPELT

These burritos are fully loaded with energy and made even more wholesome with the addition of spelt berries. We find them to be flavor packed, yet tame enough spiciness-wise to enjoy for breakfast if you prefer savory foods first thing in the morning.

2 teaspoons (10 ml) grapeseed or olive oil

¾ cup (120 g) minced yellow onion

1 bell pepper (any color), seeded and diced

1 small jalapeño pepper, seeded and minced

2 tablespoons (20 g) minced garlic

1 teaspoon smoked or regular paprika

1 teaspoon ground cumin

1 teaspoon mild to medium chili powder

½ teaspoon ground turmeric

½ teaspoon fine sea salt, to taste

1 cup (194 g) cooked spelt berries

1 can (15 ounces, or 425 g) black or kidney beans, drained and rinsed

Heaping ¾ cup (210 g) Slightly Cheesy Cashew Sauce (page 166), plus extra for serving

6 tablespoons (6 g) minced fresh cilantro

6 (8-inch, or 20 cm) vegan flour tortillas

Nonstick cooking spray or oil spray

Favorite hot sauce, for serving

Preheat the oven to 400°F (200°C, or gas mark 6).

Place the oil, onion, peppers, garlic, paprika, cumin, chili powder, turmeric, and salt in a large skillet. Cook for 4 to 6 minutes on medium-high heat, stirring frequently, until the peppers and onion just soften while remaining slightly crisp. Stir spelt and beans into the mixture. Cook another 4 minutes. Add the sauce. Simmer another 2 minutes until thickened and fragrant.

Divide the mixture among the flour tortillas (½ cup, or 125 g, per tortilla), top with 1 tablespoon (1 g) cilantro, and roll burrito-style. Lightly coat each burrito with cooking spray. Bake for 15 minutes or until light golden brown. Serve immediately with extra cheesy sauce and hot sauce. (If you prefer your burritos unbaked, warm the flour tortillas in a heated pan on medium heat, about 30 seconds on each side to soften before use. Add heated filling to each tortilla, fold burrito style, and serve immediately.)

YIELD: 6 burritos

Polenta Topped Mexi-Beans

▶ **GRAIN:** POLENTA ▶ GLUTEN-FREE POTENTIAL ▶ SOY-FREE POTENTIAL

Rice and beans, the Mexican (and vegan) mainstay, just got an upgrade. Savory, lightly sauced beans nestle under a crispy polenta round, just waiting for the salsa and avocado to make the dish complete.

1 tablespoon (15 ml) olive oil

½ cup (80 g) minced onion

3 cloves garlic, minced

1 poblano pepper, roasted and peeled, (see Recipe Note), chopped

2 teaspoons (5 g) ground cumin

1 teaspoon smoked paprika

½ teaspoon dried oregano

½ teaspoon dried thyme

½ teaspoon chili powder, or to taste

1 can (15 ounces, or 425 g) pinto beans, drained and rinsed

2 tablespoons (34 g) tomato paste

2 tablespoons (30 ml) dry red wine, or additional broth

3 tablespoons (45 ml) vegetable broth, more if needed

Salt and pepper

1 teaspoon apple cider vinegar, optional

1 recipe Mom's Polenta (page 28)

High heat neutral-flavored oil, for roasting the poblano and cooking the polenta

½ avocado, pitted, peeled, and sliced

Salsa, for serving

Heat the oil in large skillet over medium heat. Add the onion, garlic, poblano, cumin, paprika, oregano, thyme, and chili powder. Cook, stirring, for 3 to 4 minutes until fragrant. Add the beans, tomato paste, wine, and broth. Cook over low heat, stirring occasionally, for 15 minutes. If the mixture appears dry, add extra splashes of broth as needed. Season to taste with the salt and pepper. Add the vinegar, if desired.

Heat a thin layer of oil in a large skillet over medium-high heat. After lifting the polenta in the paper lining from the loaf pan, use a biscuit cutter to cut the polenta into two rounds. Pour a ¼-inch (6 mm) layer of oil in a large skillet and heat over medium heat. Add the rounds. Do not move them until the bottoms are slightly browned, about 4 to 6 minutes. Moving them too soon can remove the crisp outer coating. Turn over the rounds and cook the second side until browned and crisp, 4 to 6 minutes.

To serve, divide the beans in half between the two plates using a biscuit cutter as a mold. Gently lift the mold and add a polenta round. Top with salsa and avocado.

YIELD: 2 servings

Recipe Note

• To roast the poblano, preheat the oven to broil. Lightly coat the poblano with oil and place on a small baking sheet. Cook for 8 to 10 minutes, turning occasionally, until blackened and blistered. Put the poblano in a bowl and cover tightly with plastic wrap. Let sit for 10 minutes, and then peel the skin away with your hands. Remove the seeds and chop as desired. Follow these cues to roast any kind of pepper.

Split Pea and Rice Artichoke Mujaddara

▶ **GRAIN:** BROWN RICE ▶ SOY-FREE POTENTIAL ▶ GLUTEN-FREE POTENTIAL

We did a version of mujaddara in *The Great Vegan Protein Book*, and we love it so much that we couldn't resist whipping up a different one here. This time, we're using split peas instead of lentils, mostly because we find split peas aren't used in enough creative ways. Nothing against split pea soup, but they're too good to be restricted to that role. Here, we're combining them with long-grain brown rice. Jasmine is Celine's favorite, but basmati is great too.

⅔ cup (130 g) dry green split peas, rinsed and picked through

⅔ cup (123 g) dry long-grain brown rice, rinsed and picked through

1¼ cups (295 ml) vegetable broth

1 tablespoon (15 ml) olive oil or melted coconut oil

1 medium red onion, diced

1 jalapeño pepper, seeded and minced

Scant 2 tablespoons (15 g) minced garlic

1½ teaspoons packed, grated fresh ginger

8 ounces (227 g) chopped cooked artichoke hearts (jarred or canned)

½ teaspoon fine sea salt, to taste

½ teaspoon turmeric

½ teaspoon ground cumin

½ teaspoon ground coriander

½ teaspoon smoked paprika

Fresh cilantro or parsley leaves, to taste

Lemon wedges, to serve

Place peas in a pot, cover with an extra 2 inches (5 cm) of water, and bring to a boil. Lower the heat, partially cover with a lid, and simmer for about 30 minutes until the peas are tender. Drain, rinse, and set aside.

While the peas are cooking, place the rice in a wide, shallow pot. Cover with broth, stir to combine, and bring to a boil. Lower the heat, cover with a lid, and simmer until the rice is tender, about 30 to 35 minutes. Remove from the heat and leave covered for 10 minutes. Fluff with a fork.

While the rice is resting, in a large skillet add the oil, onion, pepper, garlic, and ginger. Cook on medium-high heat until softened, about 4 minutes, stirring occasionally. Add the artichokes, salt, turmeric, cumin, coriander, and paprika, stirring to combine. Cook for another 2 minutes. Turn off the heat. Gently fold the split peas and rice into the spices. Top with a handful of herbs and lemon wedges.

Leftovers taste even better and can be stored in an airtight container in the refrigerator for up to 4 days. Slowly reheat before serving.

YIELD: 4 servings

Einkorn Paella

▶ **GRAIN**: EINKORN ▶ SOY-FREE POTENTIAL

Our delightfully simple paella is adorned with chickpeas, but you can also brown pieces of Pepper Grain Sausages (page 87) and add them on top. Einkorn can be replaced with hulled barley, rice, or any similar grain. Just be sure to precook your pick so that only 10 minutes of cooking time remain.

¾ cup (144 g) dry einkorn, rinsed and drained

4 cups (940 ml) vegetable broth

1 tablespoon (15 ml) olive oil

2 poblanos or bell peppers (any color), seeded and diced

¾ cup (120 g) diced red onion

1½ tablespoons (15 g) minced garlic

1½ teaspoons smoked paprika

½ teaspoon (quite loose, not packed) saffron threads

½ teaspoon coarse kosher salt, to taste

½ teaspoon dried oregano leaves (not powder, use ¼ teaspoon if powder)

1 sprig fresh thyme

1 cup (134 g) frozen green peas

1½ cups (256 g) cooked chickpeas

Splash of dry vegan white wine, optional

Ground black pepper, to taste

¼ cup (15 g) chopped fresh flat-leaf parsley

Lemon wedges, for garnish

Combine the einkorn with the broth in a large pot. Bring to a boil, lower the heat to medium and precook for 20 minutes. Carefully drain the einkorn by placing a fine-mesh sieve on top of a glass bowl or measuring cup to save the cooking liquid.

While the einkorn cooks, place the oil in a large skillet along with the poblanos and onion. Sauté on medium-high heat for 2 minutes. Add the garlic and paprika. Sauté for another 2 minutes until slightly softened and lightly browned. Add saffron, salt, oregano, thyme, 1 cup (235 ml) of the reserved cooking liquid, and cooked einkorn to the poblanos, gently folding to combine. Bring to a gentle boil, lower the heat, and cover with a lid. Simmer until the einkorn is al dente, about 10 minutes, stirring occasionally. Add extra cooking liquid, if needed. Stir the peas and chickpeas into the einkorn, add a splash of wine, and cook uncovered for another 5 minutes, stirring occasionally. Discard the thyme. Adjust seasoning, if needed. Top each serving with parsley and a wedge of lemon.

YIELD: 4 servings

Berbere Kamut with Avocado

▶ **GRAIN**: KAMUT ▶ SOY-FREE POTENTIAL

Berbere is an Ethiopian spice mix with varying levels of heat, depending on the brand purchased. It's best to add it to taste so that you don't end up with too-salty or too-spicy results. Add extra berbere at the end, if needed. We love it here in this colorful and comforting kamut dish where the avocado rounds things out with its creamy richness. If kamut isn't handy, use any grain with a similar texture, such as wheat berries, whole freekeh, or spelt, adjusting cooking time accordingly (see Grain Chart, pages 15–16).

1 cup (184 g) dry kamut, rinsed and drained

4 cups (940 ml) vegetable broth

1 tablespoon (15 ml) grapeseed or olive oil

½ teaspoon coarse kosher salt, more to taste

1 generous cup (130 g) chopped carrot (about 2 carrots)

2 medium sweet potatoes, peeled and chopped

Generous ½ cup (90 g) chopped yellow onion

2 large cloves garlic, minced

2 to 2½ teaspoons (6 to 7.5 g) berbere spice, to taste

½ teaspoon ground cumin

1 tablespoon (17 g) organic tomato paste

2 large avocados (or 1 small avocado per serving), pitted, peeled, and chopped

Combine kamut with broth in a large pot. Bring to a boil, cover, and simmer until cooked al dente, about 45 to 60 minutes. Drain carefully in a fine-mesh sieve placed on top of a glass measuring cup or bowl to reserve the extra broth. Set aside.

Place the oil, salt, and carrots in a skillet fitted with a lid. Sauté for 1 minute, cover with the lid and cook for 4 minutes. Add the sweet potato, onion, garlic, spice mix to taste, cumin, and tomato paste, stirring to combine, and sauté 2 minutes. Add reserved broth as needed, 1 tablespoon (15 ml) at a time. Cover with the lid. Simmer 15 minutes or until the carrots and potatoes soften but aren't fully tender. Keep adding broth as needed. Add the cooked kamut. Simmer covered for another 10 to 15 minutes until slightly saucy and the veggies are perfectly tender but not mushy. Be sure to add reserved broth as needed. (We needed ½ cup plus 2 tablespoons, or 150 ml, in all.)

Let stand covered 15 minutes before serving. Adjust seasoning, if needed. Add chopped avocado on each portion and serve immediately.

YIELD: 4 to 6 servings

Brussels Sprouts Rice and Groats Bake

▶ GRAINS: BLACK RICE AND OAT GROATS ▶ GLUTEN-FREE POTENTIAL

This bake has turned a couple of brussels sprouts haters into new aficionados. Victory! We recommend cooking the oats and rice separately so that the purpleness the black rice releases while cooking doesn't alter the color of the oats. Use wild rice if black rice isn't available, adjusting cooking time accordingly (see Grain Chart, pages 15–16).

⅔ cup (123 g) dry oat groats, rinsed, cooked to al dente and cooled

½ cup (90 g) dry black rice, rinsed, cooked to al dente, and cooled

1 tablespoon (15 ml) grapeseed or olive oil

½ cup plus 1 tablespoon (90 g) chopped shallot

10 ounces (283 g) trimmed brussels sprouts, shaved to ⅛-inch (3 mm) thickness

3 cloves garlic, minced

2 tablespoons (30 ml) mirin

1 tablespoon (15 ml) ume plum vinegar

1¼ cups (295 ml) water, divided

1 cup (130 g) chopped carrots (yellow or white is best)

2 teaspoons (5 g) Broth Powder (page 167)

1 cup (240 g) Basic Cashew Cream (page 166)

1 tablespoon (8 g) nutritional yeast

2 teaspoons (10 ml) fresh lemon juice

1 tablespoon (18 g) white miso

1 teaspoon sriracha, to taste

1 tablespoon (5 g) minced scallion

In a skillet, place the oil and shallot and sauté on medium-high heat until translucent, about 2 minutes. Add the brussels sprouts and sauté for another 5 minutes until lightly browned. Add the garlic, mirin, vinegar, and ¼ cup (60 ml) water (less if sprouts are shaved thinner than ⅛ inch [3 mm], add as needed). Cover with a lid, and simmer until tender, about 5 minutes. Stir the cooled oats and rice into the sprouts.

Preheat the oven to 375°F (190°C, or gas mark 5). Place the sprouts mixture at the bottom of an 10 x 8-inch (25 x 20 cm) oval baking dish.

In the meantime, prepare the carrots by adding them to the remaining 1 cup (235 ml) water combined with broth powder. (You can replace this with vegetable broth.) Bring to a boil, then lower the heat to medium. Cook until fork-tender, about 12 minutes, and drain. Transfer to a food processor along with cashew cream, nutritional yeast, lemon juice, miso, and sriracha. Process until completely smooth. Pulse the scallion to combine. Evenly spread the cream mixture on top of sprouts mixture. Bake for 30 minutes until light golden brown on top. Let stand 10 minutes before serving.

YIELD: 6 to 8 servings

Butternut Bean Kamut-sotto

▶ GRAIN: KAMUT ▶ SOY-FREE POTENTIAL

It would be impossible to pick only one favorite whole grain out of all our new favorites, but kamut is a strong contender. We've paired it with leftover roasted butternut squash in this "risotto," and were quite impressed with the fancy outcome and fabulous flavors. We hope you will be, too. If kamut isn't handy, use any grain with a similar texture, such as wheat berries, whole freekeh, or spelt, adjusting cooking time accordingly (see Grain Chart, pages 15–16).

1 cup (184 g) dry kamut, rinsed and drained

4 cups (940 ml) water, divided

1 tablespoon plus 1 teaspoon (11 g) Broth Powder (page 167), divided

1½ cups (290 g) roasted bite-size butternut squash cubes (see Recipe Note)

½ cup (120 g) chipotle dressing (page 147)

½ teaspoon coarse kosher salt, to taste

1½ teaspoons grapeseed or olive oil

½ cup plus 2 tablespoons (100 g) chopped shallot

1 tablespoon (10 g) minced garlic

1 teaspoon smoked paprika

½ teaspoon ground cumin

1 can (15 ounces, or 425 g) white, black, or kidney beans, drained and rinsed

Combine kamut with 3 cups (705 ml) water and 1 tablespoon (8 g) broth powder in a large pot, and bring to a boil. Cover, and simmer until cooked al dente, about 45 to 60 minutes. Drain, if needed, and set aside.

In a blender, combine the remaining 1 cup (235 ml) water, remaining teaspoon broth powder, roasted squash, chipotle dressing, and salt. Blend until perfectly smooth.

In a skillet, combine the oil and shallot. Heat on medium-high heat and cook until fragrant and the shallot is translucent, about 4 minutes. Add the garlic, paprika, cumin, beans, and cooked kamut. Cook for another 2 minutes. Stir the blended squash sauce into the mixture, cover with a lid, and simmer for 10 to 15 minutes until heated through. Serve. Leftovers can be stored in an airtight container in the refrigerator for up to 3 days. Slowly reheat before serving.

YIELD: 4 servings

Recipe Note

To roast butternut squash, preheat the oven to 400°F (200°C, or gas mark 6). Prepare a small squash by cutting, peeling, and cubing it. Toss it with a drizzle of olive oil and salt. Arrange the cubes on a large, rimmed baking sheet. Roast until tender and browned, about 30 minutes. Roasting time will depend on the freshness of the squash and the cube size, so check occasionally.

Creamy Amaranth Polenta with Marinara

▶ **GRAIN**: AMARANTH ▶ GLUTEN-FREE POTENTIAL

There's no limit to how many bowls of creamy amaranth polenta that Celine and her husband could eat, if they let themselves. Self-control is hard! Note that if your herbes de Provence mix contains lavender or fennel, you must steer clear (the flavor combo wouldn't be great) and use Italian seasoning instead.

FOR THE MARINARA:

1½ teaspoons grapeseed or olive oil

¼ cup plus 2 tablespoons (60 g) minced shallot

2 cloves garlic, minced

1 yellow (or other color) bell pepper, seeded and diced

Salt and pepper

Red pepper flakes, to taste, optional

1 teaspoon herbes de Provence or Italian seasoning

2 cups plus 2 tablespoons (545 g) chopped tomatoes with juice (such as Pomi)

1 tablespoon (7 g) minced soft sun-dried tomatoes

1½ teaspoons capers, minced, plus extra for garnish

FOR THE POLENTA:

1 cup (180 g) dry amaranth

2 scant cups (460 ml) no- or low-salt vegetable broth or water

½ cup (60 g) chopped carrot, cooked until tender

¼ cup plus 2 tablespoons (90 g) Basic Cashew Cream (page 166)

1 tablespoon (8 g) nutritional yeast

2 teaspoons (12 g) white miso

2 teaspoons (10 ml) fresh lemon juice

1 teaspoon Broth Powder (page 167)

To make the marinara: Place the oil, shallot, garlic, and bell pepper in a skillet. Cook on medium-high heat and stir occasionally until the pepper softens, about 4 minutes. Add salt and pepper, herbes de Provence, tomatoes, and sun-dried tomatoes. Lower the heat to medium and simmer uncovered for 10 minutes. Stir the capers into the sauce. Set aside.

To make the polenta: Place the amaranth and vegetable broth (or water) in a large pot. Bring to a boil. Lower the heat to medium low, cover with a lid, and simmer for 15 minutes. Remove the lid occasionally to stir the amaranth, and adjust the heat, if needed, to prevent scorching.

In the meantime, combine the remaining ingredients in a small blender, or use a handheld blender, and blend until perfectly smooth. Fold the sauce into the amaranth after the 15 minutes cooking time. Continue to simmer covered for another 5 minutes or until thickened like polenta, or to taste. Scoop out the polenta and serve with marinara. Leftover marinara can be stored in an airtight container in the refrigerator for up to 4 days.

YIELD: 3 to 4 side-dish servings, or 2 main-dish servings, and 3 cups (about 690 g) marinara

Kamut Puttanesca

▶ GRAINS: KAMUT AND CRACKED WHEAT ▶ SOY-FREE POTENTIAL

Puttanesca is a tomato-based sauce with bold flavors. We've taken a less conventional road by using bell pepper in the preparation and a combination of whole grains to stand in for traditional pasta. Kamut tends to absorb the sauce a little less efficiently than pasta, that's why we've combined it with cracked wheat to soak up the flavor and thicken the sauce. You can substitute whole freekeh, spelt berries, triticale berries, or wheat berries for kamut, adjusting cooking time accordingly (see Grain Chart, pages 15–16).

¾ cup (138 g) dry kamut, rinsed and drained

3 cups (705 ml) vegetable broth

1 tablespoon (15 ml) olive oil

1 bell pepper (any color), trimmed and chopped

3½ tablespoons (35 g) chopped shallot

1 tablespoon (10 g) minced garlic

1 tablespoon (7 g) minced soft sun-dried tomatoes (not packed in oil)

1 tablespoon (9 g) capers (a little brine is acceptable)

10 kalamata olives, or a medley, pitted and chopped

¼ to ½ teaspoon red pepper flakes, to taste

Pinch dried basil (see Recipe Note)

1 can (15 ounces, or 425 g) fire-roasted diced tomatoes with juice

¾ cup (180 g) cooked cracked wheat or bulgur

Salt and pepper

Combine kamut with broth in a large pot and bring to a boil. Cover and simmer until cooked al dente, about 45 to 60 minutes. Drain and set aside.

Place the oil, bell pepper, shallot, and garlic in a large skillet. Sauté on medium heat until the pepper just starts to soften, about 3 minutes. Add the sun-dried tomatoes, capers, olives, red pepper flakes, and basil, stirring to combine and cooking for 1 minute. Add the diced tomatoes, stir to combine, and cover with a lid. Lower the heat and simmer for 15 minutes. Add the cooked kamut and cracked wheat, stirring to combine. Cover with the lid again. Simmer for another 5 minutes until heated through and to let the flavors meld. Adjust the seasoning, if needed. Serve as is, or with baked tempeh or tofu.

YIELD: 4 servings

Recipe Note

Fresh is always better, but Celine often has trouble finding basil that doesn't look like it went around the world in 80 days before being sold. That said, if you have a couple of beautiful leaves of fresh basil, pretty please skip using dried, and cut your basil leaves into a chiffonade just before serving, sprinkling some on each portion.

Chickpea Millet Curry

▶ GRAIN: MILLET ▶ SOY-FREE POTENTIAL ▶ QUICK AND EASY ▶ GLUTEN-FREE POTENTIAL

We love to come home to a ready-in-no-time dinner, when all we crave is healthy, filling comfort food of the whole-grain variety. This one definitely hits the spot! Millet can be replaced with any cooked cereal you love the most.

1 teaspoon melted coconut oil or grapeseed oil

Generous ¼ cup (30 g) chopped scallion

½ to 1 whole jalapeño pepper, seeded and minced, to taste

2 cloves garlic, minced

2 teaspoons (4 g) grated fresh ginger

2 teaspoons (4 g) mild to medium curry powder

½ teaspoon ground cumin

1 bell pepper (any color), seeded and diced

1½ cups (260 g) cooked millet

1 cup (164 g) cooked chickpeas

½ teaspoon fine sea salt, to taste

½ cup (120 ml) canned coconut milk

Water or vegetable broth, as needed

Chopped fresh cilantro or parsley, to taste

Wedges of lime, for garnish

Place the oil, scallion, jalapeño, garlic, ginger, curry, cumin, and bell pepper in a large skillet. Sauté on medium-high heat for about 6 minutes until the bell pepper softens. Add a drizzle of water if the veggies stick to the skillet and adjust the heat. Add the millet, chickpeas, and salt to taste. Cook on medium heat for 2 minutes. Add the milk, and simmer for 4 minutes. Add extra vegetable broth or water if the curry is too thick for your taste. Cook just to heat through. Serve immediately with fresh herbs and wedges of lime.

YIELD: 2 to 3 servings

Spelt Chili

▶ GRAIN: SPELT ▶ SOY-FREE POTENTIAL

Nothing beats a big bowl of protein-packed and flavor-filled vegan chili on colder days. As an added bonus, the spelt berries make it even heartier! If spelt isn't available, cooked kamut, wheat berries, or any grain similar in texture, and sturdy enough to endure extra cooking time will be perfect here. If you're looking for a mega boost of protein, brown some chopped pieces of your favorite seitan and add it on top. Homemade guacamole would be fantastic as well.

½ ounce (14 g) sliced dried shiitake or other mushrooms, rinsed to remove grit

1 cup (235 ml) water

1 tablespoon (15 ml) grapeseed or olive oil

½ cup plus 2 tablespoons (100 g) chopped shallot or red onion

4 cloves garlic, minced

7 ounces (200 g) mini heirloom tomatoes, halved or quartered depending on size (or 1 cup, or 240 g, canned fire-roasted diced tomatoes)

2 small bell peppers, seeded and diced (any color)

1 small jalapeño pepper, seeded and minced

2 tablespoons (33 g) tomato paste

2 tablespoons (15 g) mild to medium chili powder

2 teaspoons (5 g) ground cumin

½ teaspoon fine sea salt, to taste

¼ cup (30 g) nutritional yeast

1 tablespoon (8 g) Broth Powder (page 167)

1 can (15 ounces, or 420 g) tomato sauce (reserve the can)

1⅓ cups (253 g) cooked spelt berries

1½ cups (257 g) cooked black beans

Place the mushrooms in a medium bowl. Add the water on top, and press on the mushrooms to make sure they absorb the liquid. Soak for 5 minutes. Gently squeeze the liquid out of the mushrooms and set aside. Mince the mushrooms and set aside.

In a large-size pot, place the oil, shallot, garlic, tomatoes, and all peppers. Heat over medium heat and sauté for 4 to 6 minutes until the vegetables just start to soften. Stir occasionally. Add the tomato paste, chili powder, cumin, and salt. Cook for 1 minute. Add the mushrooms, nutritional yeast, broth powder, and tomato sauce. Pour the reserved mushroom liquid in the empty tomato sauce can. Add enough filtered water to reach the top edge of the can. Pour into the pot. Bring to a gentle boil, cover with a lid. Lower the heat and simmer for 15 minutes. Add the cooked spelt and beans, and simmer another 10 to 15 minutes until thickened to your liking. Reheated leftovers taste even better, as is so often the case with such dishes.

YIELD: 6 servings

Ras el Hanout Millet

▶ GRAIN: MILLET ▶ SOY-FREE POTENTIAL ▶ QUICK AND EASY ▶ GLUTEN-FREE POTENTIAL

Ras el hanout is a rich, Moroccan spice blend composed of ingredients such as coriander, turmeric, cardamom, and more. It can be purchased online or at well-stocked or international markets. We love it in this beautifully flavored, pilaflike dish that proves once again that millet should be placed in the spotlight more often. One of our testers (Liz) served it with a lightly dressed red cabbage salad, and we can concur that it's a mighty fine pairing.

½ cup (110 g) dry millet, rinsed and drained

1 cup (235 ml) vegetable broth

1½ cups (246 g) cooked chickpeas

¼ cup (40 g) golden raisins (not packed) or (36 g) dried black currants

1 tablespoon (15 ml) toasted sesame oil

1¼ cups (140 g) finely grated carrot (about 2 medium carrots)

6 tablespoons (35 g) chopped scallion (white and green parts)

1 large clove garlic, grated or pressed

1½ teaspoons ras el hanout

¼ teaspoon red pepper flakes, to taste (optional)

½ teaspoon coarse kosher salt, to taste

Sumac, for garnish (or freshly grated zest from 1 large organic lemon)

Fresh cilantro, mint, or parsley leaves, for garnish

Chopped or whole pistachios, for garnish, optional

For even better results, take a moment to toast the millet in a skillet (page 8). Combine the millet and broth in a large skillet. Bring to a boil, lower the heat, cover with a lid and simmer until the liquid is absorbed, about 15 minutes. Remove from the heat and let stand 2 minutes. Fluff with a fork and set aside.

While the millet is cooking, combine the chickpeas, raisins, oil, carrot, scallion, garlic, ras el hanout, red pepper flakes, and salt in another large skillet.

Sauté on medium-high heat, stirring often, until the scallion soften slightly and the mixture is fragrant, about 5 minutes. Gently fold the millet into the chickpeas. Cook another 2 minutes, stirring occasionally.

This dish can be served immediately or left to stand at room temperature for 30 minutes before serving. Right before serving, garnish each portion with a pinch of sumac (or lemon zest), fresh herb of choice, and pistachios, if using.

YIELD: 4 servings

Tempeh Buckwheat Bowl

▶ **GRAIN**: BUCKWHEAT ▶ GLUTEN-FREE POTENTIAL

We've combined some of our favorite Eastern flavors to create a light peanut sauce, and it plays very well with the protein-dense tempeh and vegetables. The peanut sauce is light, but layered, making this one a pleaser!

PEANUTTY SAUCE:

1 teaspoon neutral-flavored oil

¼ cup (40 g) chopped onion

2 cloves garlic, minced

½ teaspoon minced fresh ginger

1 teaspoon ground cumin

½ teaspoon ground coriander

½ teaspoon five-spice powder

⅔ cup (160 ml) vegetable broth

2 tablespoons (32 g) smooth peanut butter

1 tablespoon (15 ml) seasoned rice vinegar

1 tablespoon (15 ml) tamari

1 to 2 teaspoons (5 to 10 g) sambal oelek

Salt and pepper

TEMPEH AND BUCKWHEAT:

2 tablespoons (30 ml) high heat neutral-flavored oil

8 ounces (227 g) tempeh, cut into ½-inch (1.3 cm) pieces (See Recipe Note)

1 cup (100 g) small cauliflower florets

2 teaspoons (5 g) ground cumin

1 teaspoon five-spice powder

¾ cup (135 g) dry buckwheat groats, cooked, rinsed in cold water, and cooled

⅓ cup (30 g) (1-inch, or 2.5 cm) pieces snow peas

¼ cup (25 g) chopped scallion

1 carrot, shredded

Salt and pepper

To make the peanutty sauce: Heat the oil in a small skillet over medium heat. Add the onion, garlic, and ginger. Cook, stirring occasionally, for 5 minutes until fragrant. Add the cumin, coriander, and five-spice powder, and cook 2 minutes longer. Add the broth, peanut butter, vinegar, tamari, and sambal oelek. Stir occasionally and bring to a boil then remove from the heat. Transfer to a small high-powered blender and process until smooth. Pour back into the skillet but do not place on the heat.

To make the tempeh and buckwheat: Heat the oil in large skillet over medium heat. Add the tempeh and cauliflower. Cook, stirring occasionally, for 5 to 7 minutes until the tempeh is browned. Add the cumin and five-spice powder. Cook for 2 minutes. Add the buckwheat, snow peas, scallion, and carrot. Cook, for 5 minutes, stirring frequently, until heated throughout and combined. Season to taste with salt and pepper.

Reheat the sauce over low heat, if necessary. Season to taste with salt and pepper. Divide the tempeh and buckwheat mixture evenly between 4 bowls. Drizzle evenly with the sauce.

YIELD: 4 servings, scant 1 cup sauce (200 g)

Recipe Note

Some people find tempeh to have a bitter taste. To counter that, simmer the block of tempeh in water for 20 minutes and then drain. Continue with the recipe.

Creamy Pesto Asparagus Einkorn

▶ GRAIN: EINKORN ▶ SOY-FREE POTENTIAL

We're suckers for anything that contains homemade pesto or fresh asparagus, so coming up with a dish that would highlight one of our new favorite whole grains (einkorn), and contain both the aforementioned, felt more like a vacation than work. Hulled barley or brown rice would be good alternatives here if einkorn plays hard to get. We must warn you that this is a dish best served fresh, as any grain will continue to absorb the pesto once refrigerated. If you have leftovers be sure to add a little extra pesto upon reheating.

¾ cup (144 g) dry einkorn, rinsed and drained

1½ cups (355 ml) vegetable broth

12 ounces (340 g) trimmed thin green asparagus, roasted or steamed (see Recipe Note)

½ cup (65 g) thinly sliced red onion

¼ cup (60 g) Basic Cashew Cream (page 166)

¼ cup (60 g) pesto (page 105) or other favorite vegan pesto, more to taste

Salt and pepper

Chopped fresh parsley, for garnish

Place the einkorn and broth in a medium saucepan. Bring to a boil. Lower the heat, cover with a lid, and simmer until al dente, 30 to 35 minutes. While the einkorn is cooking, chop the prepared asparagus into 1-inch (2.5 cm) pieces and add to a large skillet. Fold the cashew cream and pesto into the asparagus. During the last 5 minutes of cooking time for the einkorn, add the onion to the boiling water to soften. Drain the einkorn. Stir the einkorn into the asparagus, adjust seasoning to taste, and simmer covered for another 5 minutes. For extra flavor and creaminess, add more pesto to taste. Garnish each serving with parsley.

YIELD: 4 servings

Recipe Notes

- You can roast the asparagus or sauté them in a pan until just tender if you don't mind the extra little bit of oil roasting and sautéing involved. Preheat the oven to 400°F (200°C, or gas mark 6). Place the asparagus on a rimmed baking sheet, and lightly drizzle with 2 teaspoons (10 ml) olive oil. Sprinkle with a pinch of salt. Roast for 10 minutes or until tender yet crisp.

- For a no-fat method, steam the asparagus instead until tender yet crisp.

Einkorn and Roasted Root Vegetable Gratin

▶ **GRAIN**: EINKORN

It's so easy to fall in love with einkorn's fantastic texture and mildly nutty flavor in this colorful gratin, but einkorn can be a little costly and occasionally hard to find. The more affordable doppelganger we recommend here is cooked hulled barley or medium- or long-grain brown rice. Be sure to follow the cooking instructions specific to the alternative grain you pick!

¾ cup (144 g) dry einkorn, rinsed and drained

1½ cups (355 ml) vegetable broth

3 medium turnips, trimmed and peeled, cut into ¾-inch (2 cm) cubes

3 medium yellow carrots, trimmed and peeled, cut into 1-inch (2.5 cm) pieces, halved lengthwise if thick

1 ounce (28 g, about 5 large) peeled cloves garlic, left whole

2.8 ounces (80 g, about 1 medium to large) peeled and trimmed shallot, quartered

1 tablespoon plus 2 teaspoons (25 ml) grapeseed or olive oil, divided

¾ teaspoon coarse kosher salt, divided

¾ teaspoon smoked paprika, divided

1 tablespoon (8 g) Broth Powder (page 167), divided

3 medium red beets, trimmed and peeled, cut into ¾-inch (1.9 cm) cubes

1¼ cups (303 g) Slightly Cheesy Cashew Sauce (page 166, made with a pinch of smoked paprika), prepared and cooked to thicken slightly

Place the einkorn and broth in a medium saucepan. Bring to a boil. Lower the heat, cover with a lid, and simmer until al dente or to taste, 30 to 35 minutes. Set aside.

Preheat the oven to 400°F (200°C, or gas mark 6). Have two 8-inch (20 cm) baking dishes ready. (You're roasting separately so that the beets don't stain the other vegetables.)

In one of the dishes, combine turnips, carrots, garlic, shallot, along with 1 tablespoon (15 ml) oil, ½ teaspoon each salt and paprika, and 2 teaspoons (5 g) broth powder. In the second dish, combine beets, remaining 2 teaspoons (10 ml) oil, ¼ teaspoon each salt and paprika, and 1 teaspoon broth powder. Bake for 40 minutes or until the vegetables are just fork tender, stirring occasionally. Remove from oven. Lower the heat to 350°F (180°C, or gas mark 4).

Place cooked einkorn at the bottom of an 8 x 10-inch (20 x 25 cm) oval baking dish. Chop the shallot and garlic once cool enough to handle. Place the vegetables evenly on top of einkorn. Pour sauce evenly on top. Bake for 15 minutes. Let stand 10 minutes before serving.

YIELD: 6 servings

Roasted Radish Freekeh Bowl with Mustard Miso Sauce

▶ **GRAIN:** FREEKEH

Radishes take on a special mellowness in this dish. When roasted alongside broccoli, you just know this will be as much of a feast for your taste buds as it is for your eyes. The oil-free sauce is rich and flavorful. If you have extra, it can be refrigerated airtight for 3 days and used as a salad dressing. Other grain options? Try barley, einkorn, farro, or cracked freekeh.

½ cup (90 g) dry whole freekeh

1 bunch (8 ounces, or 227 g) radishes, cleaned, cut into ½-inch (1.3 cm) cubes

2½ cups (5 ounces, or 142 g) broccoli florets

1 tablespoon (15 ml) olive oil

Salt and pepper

⅓ cup (80 ml) vegetable broth

2 tablespoons (18 g) raw cashews

1 tablespoon (15 g) Dijon mustard

1 tablespoon (15 ml) apple cider vinegar

2 teaspoons (12 g) dark miso

1 teaspoon prepared horseradish

1 teaspoon pure maple syrup

Put the freekeh in a saucepan and cover with 4 inches (10 cm) of water. Bring to a boil, then cover, and reduce to simmer for 40 minutes or until tender. Set aside.

Heat the oven to 400°F (200°C, or gas mark 6). Combine the radishes, broccoli, and oil in a 9 x 13-inch (23 x 33 cm) pan. Season with salt and pepper. Roast for 30 minutes. When done, transfer to a medium-size bowl. Add the freekeh and stir to combine.

To make the sauce, combine the broth, cashews, mustard, vinegar, miso, horseradish, and maple syrup in a small high-powered blender. Process until smooth.

Divide the freekeh mixture between two plates. Drizzle with the sauce as desired.

YIELD: 2 servings, ⅔ cup (160 ml) sauce

Apple Butter Einkorn Sloppy Joes

▶ **GRAIN**: EINKORN

Hulled barley can be subbed for the einkorn if the latter is hard to find. Either grain will work wonderfully in this hearty, winter-style dish. Just be sure to adjust the cooking time accordingly (see pages 15–16). We personally love this most when piled high on baked regular or sweet potatoes. The fact that it is a fairly low-fat and high-fiber dish is an added bonus no one seems to mind.

⅓ cup (64 g) dry einkorn, rinsed and drained

⅓ cup (59 g) dry green lentils, rinsed and drained

1 tablespoon (8 g) Broth Powder (page 167)

1 teaspoon grapeseed or olive oil

¾ cup (120 g) minced red onion

1 red bell pepper, seeded and diced

2 cloves garlic, minced

¾ cup (180 g) unsweetened apple butter

½ cup (136 g) organic ketchup

1 teaspoon apple cider vinegar

1 teaspoon mild Dijon mustard

1 teaspoon vegan Worcestershire sauce

1 teaspoon liquid smoke

⅛ to ¼ teaspoon cayenne pepper, to taste (optional)

½ teaspoon fine sea salt

Vegan buns, or baked potatoes (regular or sweet), or cooked greens, for serving

Place einkorn and lentils in a pot, cover with an extra 2 to 3 inches (5 to 7.5 cm) water and broth powder. Bring to a boil, partially cover with a lid, lower the heat to medium-low, and simmer until fully tender, about 35 minutes. Drain and set aside.

Place the oil, onion, bell pepper, and garlic in a skillet. Sauté on medium heat until the onion and pepper soften, about 6 minutes, stirring occasionally. In a small bowl, whisk to combine apple butter, ketchup, vinegar, mustard, Worcestershire sauce, liquid smoke, cayenne pepper, and salt. Add to the skillet, stirring to combine. Simmer uncovered for 15 minutes, stirring occasionally. Fold the cooked einkorn and lentils into the sauce, and simmer for another 5 minutes. Let stand 10 to 15 minutes before serving. Serve the traditional way inside buns, or go off the beaten path by serving on baked potatoes or on a bed of cooked greens.

YIELD: 6 to 8 servings

Rye Shakshuka

▶ **GRAIN**: RYE BERRIES

Rye berries bring great texture and thickness to this tomato-based dish that traditionally contains poached eggs. If rye berries aren't available, use any grain with a similar texture, such as wheat berries, whole freekeh, or spelt, adjusting cooking time accordingly (see Grain Chart, pages 15–16).

½ cup (90 g) dry rye berries, rinsed and drained, cooked to al dente

1½ tablespoons (23 ml) grapeseed or olive oil, divided

1⅓ cups (200 g) chopped red bell pepper (about 2)

¼ cup (40 g) minced shallot

1 generous tablespoon (12 g) minced garlic

2 teaspoons (4 g) dry harissa blend or harissa paste, to taste

½ teaspoon ground cumin

Couple pinches of salt, to taste

1 tablespoon (17 g) tomato paste

1 can (28 ounces, or 794 g) crushed plum tomatoes

12 ounces (340 g) super-firm cubed tofu or 1½ cups (246 g) cooked chickpeas

¼ teaspoon black salt (kala namak)

¼ teaspoon smoked paprika

¼ teaspoon ground turmeric

Vegan pita or lavash bread, for serving

Follow instructions in the grain chart to cook the rye berries. Set aside.

In a large skillet, place 1 tablespoon (15 ml) oil, bell pepper, shallot, garlic, and sauté on medium-high heat for 2 minutes. Add the spices, salt, and tomato paste. Sauté for 1 minute or until the pepper starts to soften. Add the tomatoes. Lower the heat and partially cover with a lid once the mixture gets bubbly. Simmer for 10 minutes, stirring occasionally.

Place the remaining 1½ teaspoons oil in another skillet. Add the tofu cubes and sauté on medium-high heat until golden brown, about 8 minutes, stirring occasionally. Add black salt, paprika, and turmeric, and sauté 1 minute. If using chickpeas instead, sauté with spices for 4 minutes until heated through and fragrant.

Add the cooked rye to the shakshuka, stirring to combine, and partially cover with a lid. Simmer for 10 minutes, stirring occasionally. Remove the lid and place tofu or chickpeas evenly on top, without stirring. Cover and let stand 5 minutes with the stove turned off. Serve with bread.

YIELD: 6 servings

Recipe Notes

- The results are moderately spicy. Adjust the quantity of harissa as needed.

- If you don't feel like eating bread to sop up the sauce, double the quantity of rye berries for less saucy results.

Moroccan Wheat Berries

▶ **GRAIN**: WHEAT BERRIES ▶ SOY-FREE POTENTIAL

Don't let the eclectic mix of spices scare you away from this delectable concoction! Sumac is a ground, Middle Eastern berry. If you haven't tried it, you'll be smitten with its tart, lemony flavor. Kamut, spelt, triticale berries, or any similar grain can be subbed for the wheat berries. Simply adjust cooking times accordingly.

½ cup (100 g) dry chana dal, rinsed and drained

2½ tablespoons (20 g) Broth Powder (page 167), divided

¼ cup plus 2 tablespoons (72 g) dry, soft, white wheat berries, rinsed and drained

1¾ cups (224 g) minced carrot

1 tablespoon (15 ml) melted coconut oil

½ cup (80 g) minced shallot or red onion

½ teaspoon fine sea salt, to taste

1 teaspoon ground coriander

1 teaspoon ground cumin

½ teaspoon ground sumac

¼ teaspoon ground allspice

¼ teaspoon ground nutmeg

¼ teaspoon ground ginger

⅛ to ¼ teaspoon cayenne pepper, to taste

⅛ teaspoon ground cinnamon

3 cloves garlic, grated or pressed (roasted is good here if handy)

1 to 2 teaspoons (2 to 4 g) dry harissa blend or paste, to taste

1½ cups (240 g, or 1 large) diced tomato

Drizzle of fresh lemon juice, optional

Minced fresh mint, for garnish, optional

Place chana dal in a pot, cover with an extra 3 inches (7.5 cm) water and 1 tablespoon (8 g) broth powder. Bring to a boil, partially cover with a lid, lower the heat, and simmer until fully tender, about 1 hour. Drain if needed, and set aside.

At the same time, place the wheat berries in a pot, cover with an extra 3 inches (5 cm) water and 1 tablespoon (8 g) broth powder. Bring to a boil, partially cover with a lid, lower the heat, and simmer until tender, about 1 hour. Slowly and carefully drain by placing a fine-mesh sieve on top of a glass bowl or measuring cup to save the cooking liquid.

Cook carrots and shallot in oil on medium heat until softened, about 8 minutes. Stir occasionally. In the mean-time, prepare the spice mix (salt through cinnamon) in a small bowl. Add spice mix, remaining 1½ teaspoons broth powder, garlic, harissa, tomato, wheat berries, and chana dal to the skillet. Cover and cook on medium-low heat for 10 minutes to meld the flavors. Add reserved broth, if needed, or a drizzle of lemon juice. Turn off the heat, and let stand covered for 10 minutes before serving.

YIELD: 4 servings

Einkorn Succotash

▶ **GRAIN:** EINKORN ▶ SOY-FREE POTENTIAL

Succotash is a Native American dish composed of corn and lima beans, and its summery yellow and green colors are as appealing as its flavors! The einkorn can be replaced with the same amount of hulled barley or brown rice, if desired. Adjust cooking method and time according to the subbed grain. If you like spiciness, we highly recommend stirring some harissa, cayenne pepper, or any other favorite source of heat into each serving.

¾ cup (144 g) dry einkorn, rinsed and drained

2 cups (470 ml) vegetable broth

1½ teaspoons toasted sesame oil

½ cup (80 g) minced shallot

2 large cloves garlic, grated or pressed

½ green bell pepper, diced

1 cup (164 g) frozen baby lima beans, rinsed to thaw slightly

1 cup (164 g) frozen sweet white corn, rinsed to thaw slightly

Fine sea salt, to taste

Ground white peppercorn, to taste

¾ cup (110 g) marinated yellow squash and zucchini (see Recipe Note), drained (optional)

Minced fresh parsley, to taste

Place the einkorn and broth in a medium saucepan. Bring to a boil. Lower the heat, cover with a lid, and simmer until al dente, 30 to 35 minutes. Drain, if needed, and set aside.

Place the oil, shallot, garlic, bell pepper, and lima beans in a large skillet. Cook on medium-high heat until just softened, about 4 minutes. Add the corn, salt, and pepper, and sauté another 2 minutes. Add the cooked einkorn, and cook on medium-low heat until heated through, about 4 minutes. Add the marinated veggies, and sauté another 4 minutes to let the flavors meld. Adjust seasoning, if needed. Garnish each serving with parsley.

YIELD: 4 servings

Recipe Note

To prepare marinated squash and zucchini, use a vegetable peeler to shave rounds from 1 trimmed medium zucchini and 1 trimmed medium yellow squash. Combine in a medium bowl with ⅓ cup (80 ml) seasoned rice vinegar and 1 minced clove of garlic. Stir well and transfer to a large canning jar, shaking to combine once closed airtight. Store in the refrigerator for at least 1 day before use. Use within a week.

Roasted Cabbage Steaks with Chimichurri Sauce

▶ GRAIN: FREEKEH ▶ SOY-FREE POTENTIAL

Chimichurri, an Argentinian green (or occasionally red) sauce, brings a wonderfully spicy edge to a simple freekeh recipe. The sweet, roasted cabbage completes this autumn meal. If you prefer, try cracked freekeh, einkorn, farro, or kamut instead of the whole freekeh, changing the cooking times to fit the grain.

FOR THE CHIMICHURRI SAUCE:

1 bunch (3 ounces, or 85 g) fresh parsley

1 large fresh cayenne pepper or other hot pepper

1 cup (160 g) chopped onion

4 to 6 cloves garlic

2 teaspoons (4 g) dried oregano

1 teaspoon fine sea salt

½ teaspoon ground black pepper

3 tablespoons (45 ml) white wine vinegar

2 teaspoons (10 ml) olive oil

FOR THE FREEKEH AND STEAKS:

1 cup (160 g) dry whole freekeh

4 slices (½-inch, or 1.3 cm) cabbage (see Recipe Note)

2 teaspoons (10 ml) olive oil

½ teaspoon smoked salt or garlic salt

Pinch of ground black pepper

To make the chimichurri sauce: Put the parsley, hot pepper, onion, garlic, oregano, salt, and pepper into a food processor. Add the vinegar and the olive oil. Process to combine.

To make the freekeh and steaks: Put the freekeh in a saucepan and cover with 4 inches (10 cm) water. Bring to a boil, then cover, and reduce to simmer for 40 minutes or until tender. Heat the oven to 400°F (200°C, or gas mark 6). Put the cabbage slices on a large, oiled baking sheet. Using your fingers, spread ½ teaspoon of oil on each slice. Sprinkle evenly with the salt and pepper. Bake for 30 minutes. If some of the outer edges of the leaves brown, carefully cut them off.

To serve, put a slice of cabbage on each plate. Top with one-quarter of the freekeh and drizzle with the chimichurri sauce to taste.

YIELD: 4 servings, ¼ cup (60 ml) chimichurri sauce

Recipe Note

We're not going to fib. It's not easy to cut an even slice of cabbage. Our favorite method is to cut around the cabbage to make a pattern for the ½-inch (1.3 cm) slice. After going all the way around, guide your knife straight through the cabbage for a (hopefully) even slice.

Pepper Lovers' Polenta
with Raspberry BBQ Seitan

▶ GRAIN: POLENTA ▶ SOY-FREE POTENTIAL

Our supereasy raspberry BBQ sauce brings out all the flavor of the crispy polenta triangles and makes for a hearty meal. This polenta is mildly spiced as written, but rev up your engines and double the peppers, if you've got the nerve. Try it this way once, then go for the spice!

FOR THE POLENTA:

1½ cups (355 ml) water

½ cup (70 g) dry polenta

1 tablespoon (9 g) minced jalapeño pepper

1 teaspoon minced habañero pepper, more to taste

½ teaspoon onion powder

½ teaspoon fine sea salt

Ground black pepper

High heat neutral-flavored oil, for cooking

FOR THE SEITAN AND SAUCE:

¾ cup (95 g) fresh raspberries

¼ teaspoon ground allspice, plus a pinch

¼ teaspoon cayenne pepper

¼ teaspoon dried thyme

½ cup (125 g) prepared barbecue sauce

2 (4 ounces, or 113 g each) Quit-the-Cluck Seitan cutlets (page 169)

¼ teaspoon paprika

5 ounces (142 g) baby spinach

Salt and pepper

High heat neutral-flavored oil, for cooking

To make the polenta: Line a loaf pan with parchment paper, being sure to reach about 2 inches (5 cm) up the sides.

Bring the water to a boil in a medium-size saucepan over high heat. Whisk in the polenta, hot peppers, onion powder, salt, and a generous pinch of ground black pepper. Reduce the heat to simmer. Continue whisking for 5 to 10 minutes until the mixture is thick and clears the bottom of the pan. Pour into the prepared loaf pan and let cool for 30 minutes. Refrigerate for a minimum of 2 hours so the polenta is very firm. At this stage, if wrapped airtight and refrigerated, the polenta can be stored for up to 1 week.

To cook the polenta, lift the parchment paper carefully from the loaf pan. The polenta will be in a loaf-shaped plank. Cut the polenta in half vertically, then cut each half diagonally to create 4 triangles. Pour a ¼-inch (6 mm) layer of oil in a large skillet and heat over medium heat. Add the triangles and do not move them until the bottom is slightly browned, about 4 to 6 minutes. Moving them too soon can remove the crisp outer coating. Turn over the triangles, and cook the second side until browned and crisp, about 4 to 6 minutes. Serve hot.

To make the seitan and sauce: Rub the paprika and remaining pinch of allspice into one side of each cutlet. Sprinkle with salt and pepper. Oil a grill pan and heat over medium-high heat. Put the cutlets in the pan and cook until marked, 4 to 5 minutes. Turn over to cook the second side for 4 to 5 minutes or until marked.

For the sauce, purée the raspberries and pour into a small saucepan. Add ¼ teaspoon allspice, cayenne pepper, thyme, and the barbecue sauce. Stir to combine. Heat gently over low heat, then set aside until serving. Reheat, if needed.

To serve, heat a large skillet over medium heat. Quickly cook the spinach until barely wilted. Divide the spinach evenly between two plates. Top each with a seitan cutlet and 2 polenta triangles. Top with the barbecue sauce, as desired.

YIELD: 2 servings

Muhammara Redux with Sorghum

▶ GRAIN: SORGHUM ▶ SOY-FREE POTENTIAL ▶ QUICK AND EASY

Muhammara is a Middle Eastern red pepper dip, composed of walnuts, pomegranate molasses, bread crumbs, and more. We've deconstructed the dish here using pepper-based sausages and substituting whole grains for bread crumbs. While the (delicious) resulting flavor isn't entirely muhammara-like, it is a looker of a dish that can be ready relatively quickly, provided the sausages and grain were cooked ahead of time.

1 tablespoon (15 ml) olive oil, divided

2 Pepper Grain Sausages (page 87), cut into slanted, bite-size half-moons

1 tablespoon (15 ml) pomegranate molasses (see Recipe Note), plus extra for garnish

¼ cup (40 g) chopped shallot or red onion

10 ounces (283 g) shaved brussels sprouts

2 cloves garlic, grated or pressed

1 teaspoon dry harissa blend or paste, to taste

½ teaspoon ground cumin

¼ cup (60 ml) vegetable broth

Salt and pepper

Scant 1½ cups (225 g) cooked sorghum or other grain

Toasted walnuts halves, for garnish

Pomegranate seeds (arils), for garnish, optional

Fresh mint leaves or parsley, for garnish, optional

In a large skillet, heat 1½ teaspoons of oil on medium-high heat. Add the sausage pieces, and sauté until browned, stirring occasionally, about 6 minutes. Pour the molasses on top, and cook 1 minute to glaze. Transfer to a plate and set aside.

In the same skillet, place the remaining 1½ teaspoons of oil and shallot and sauté on medium-high heat until translucent, about 2 minutes. Add the sprouts, and sauté for another 5 minutes, until lightly browned. Add the garlic, harissa, cumin, and broth, cover with a lid, and simmer until tender, about 5 minutes. Stir the sorghum and sausage into the sprouts, and cook uncovered until heated through, about 2 minutes. Top each serving with walnuts, pomegranate seeds, and herb of choice. Drizzle a little extra molasses on top, if desired.

YIELD: 2 to 3 servings

Recipe Note

If you cannot purchase pomegranate molasses from your local international food store or online, make your own. Place 2 cups (470 ml) unsweetened pomegranate juice in a medium pot, bring to a low boil, lower the heat and simmer uncovered until reduced to ¼ cup plus 2 tablespoons (90 ml) for about 30 minutes. Store leftovers in an airtight jar for up to 1 week. Use on roasted vegetables, baked tofu, or salads. We also highly recommend the recipe available on www.simplyrecipes.com.

Chana Dal Dalia

▶ **GRAIN:** CRACKED WHEAT ▶ SOY-FREE POTENTIAL

Dalia is a Hindi term that refers to broken grains. It is also a porridge-like dish that is frequently served in India when illness strikes, due to its nutritional benefits as well as its blandness. We've broken tradition (and grain!) here by making things a bit more flavor rich, a little less porridge-like, and by using chana dal (split baby chickpeas) alongside cracked wheat. Serve with roasted broccoli and chapati bread.

3 cups (705 ml) water, divided

½ cup (100 g) dry chana dal (split baby chickpeas), rinsed and drained

1½ teaspoons melted coconut oil

¼ cup (40 g) chopped shallot

2 large cloves garlic, minced

1½ teaspoons grated ginger

1 small jalapeño pepper, seeded and minced

1 teaspoon ground cumin

½ teaspoon turmeric

½ teaspoon coarse kosher salt, more to taste

2 Roma tomatoes, seeded if desired, diced

½ cup (80 g) dry cracked wheat, roasted (see Recipe Note)

½ cup (8 g) chopped fresh cilantro leaves, for garnish

Combine 1½ cups (355 ml) water with chana dal in a medium pot. Bring to a boil, lower the heat, cover with a lid, and precook for 25 minutes until partially tender. (For an almost mushy Chana Dal Dalia, extend the precooking time to tender, about 30 to 35 minutes.) Drain, if needed. Set aside.

In a skillet, heat the oil on medium. Add the shallot, garlic, ginger, and jalapeño. Sauté until softened and fragrant, about 3 minutes. Add the cumin, turmeric, salt, and tomatoes, and sauté another minute. Add the roasted wheat, precooked chana dal, and remaining 1½ cups (355 ml) water, stirring to combine. Cover with a lid and cook until the water is absorbed and the wheat and chana dal are fully tender, about 30 to 35 minutes. Add extra liquid and cook longer, if needed.

Let stand 10 minutes before serving. Serve topped with cilantro. Leftovers can be stored in an airtight container in the refrigerator for up to 4 days.

YIELD: 4 servings

Recipe Note

To roast dry cracked wheat, heat a skillet on medium heat, add the cracked wheat, and slowly cook until toasted and fragrant, stirring constantly. Adjust the heat, if needed, so as not to burn the wheat. This should take about 4 minutes. Some of the cracked wheat kernels will turn white in spots, a little like popcorn. It's important to roast the cracked wheat properly so that it gets tender while cooking.

Saucy Peanut Eggplant and Freekeh

▸ **GRAIN**: FREEKEH (WHOLE) ▸ SOY-FREE POTENTIAL

We find that this easy, comforting meal is really good served on top of any type of sturdy grain. If you cannot find freekeh, use kamut, wheat berries, sorghum, or even brown rice (as gluten-free potential options), or any similar grain you love the most! Just remember to adjust cooking liquid amounts and cooking times accordingly. We should mention we rarely peel eggplant but if the skin bothers you, don't hesitate to remove it.

1 cup (160 g) dry whole freekeh, rinsed and drained

3½ cups (825 ml) water, divided, more if needed

2 tablespoons (16 g) Broth Powder (page 167), divided

½ cup plus 2 tablespoons (100 g) chopped shallot

1 eggplant, trimmed and cut into bite-size pieces

1 tablespoon (15 ml) fresh lime juice

Generous ¼ teaspoon fine sea salt, to taste

1½ tablespoons (15 g) minced garlic

1½ teaspoons grated fresh ginger, or scant ½ teaspoon ground ginger

1 to 2 teaspoons (2 to 4 g) dry harissa blend or paste, to taste

1 teaspoon ground cumin

⅓ cup (85 g) natural crunchy peanut butter

3 tablespoons (48 g) tomato paste

Fresh cilantro or parsley, for garnish

Place the freekeh, 2½ cups (590 ml) water, and 1 tablespoon (8 g) broth powder in a large pot. Bring to a boil. Lower the heat, cover with a lid, and simmer until tender, about 40 minutes. Drain, if needed, and set aside.

While the freekeh is cooking, place the shallot, eggplant, remaining 1 tablespoon (8 g) broth powder, lime juice, and salt in a large skillet. Cook on medium heat until browned, stirring frequently, about 8 minutes. If the eggplant sticks to the pan, add water or broth as needed, 1 tablespoon (15 ml) at a time.

In a medium bowl, whisk to combine the garlic, ginger, harissa, cumin, ¾ cup (180 ml) water, peanut butter, and tomato paste. Add this mixture to the eggplant. Bring to a gentle boil. Lower the heat again, cover with a lid, and simmer until the eggplant is just tender, but not mushy, about 15 to 20 minutes. The timing will depend on the freshness and size of the eggplant cubes, so be sure to check and stir occasionally to see if you need to add the remaining ¼ cup (60 ml) water to obtain the desired saucy texture. Adjust seasoning, if needed. Serve the freekeh with the eggplant preparation on top. Garnish with cilantro.

YIELD: 4 servings

Hearty Sweet Potato and Sorghum Curry

▶ **GRAIN**: SORGHUM ▶ **SOY-FREE POTENTIAL** ▶ **GLUTEN-FREE POTENTIAL**

We love to serve this dish with a side of leafy greens for a deliciously filling meal. If you prefer, you can also directly wilt 1½ cups (weight will vary) packed, finely minced greens in the curried mixture during the last 5 minutes of cooking.

1 cup (204 g) dry sorghum, soaked overnight, rinsed and drained

1¼ cups (200 g) chopped yellow onion

21 ounces (595 g) chopped sweet potato (bite-size pieces, about 4 medium potatoes)

4 cloves garlic, minced

2 tablespoons (30 ml) fresh lime juice

1 tablespoon (6 g) mild or medium curry powder

1 tablespoon (8 g) Broth Powder (page 167)

½ teaspoon ground coriander

½ teaspoon dry harissa blend or paste, more to taste

½ teaspoon fine sea salt, to taste

¼ teaspoon ground ginger

¼ teaspoon ground cumin

1 can (14 ounces, or 414 ml) full-fat coconut milk

Fresh cilantro leaves, for garnish

Place the soaked sorghum in a large pot, and cover with about 2 to 3 inches (5 to 7.5 cm) of water or vegetable broth. Bring to a boil, and cook until thoroughly tender (sorghum should not remain chewy like kamut or wheat berries), about 1 hour. Drain, and set aside.

In the meantime, cook the sweet potatoes: In a large skillet, place the onion, sweet potato, garlic, lime juice, curry powder, broth powder, coriander, harissa, salt, ginger, and cumin. Cook on medium heat until the onion and sweet potato soften slightly, about 8 minutes. Stir occasionally. If the potatoes stick to the skillet, add water, 1 tablespoon (15 ml) at a time. Add the coconut milk, bring to a gentle boil, lower the heat, and cover with a lid. Simmer until the sweet potatoes are fork tender, about 25 minutes. Cooking time depends on the size of the potato pieces, so check and stir occasionally. Adjust seasoning, if needed, adding extra harissa if you like spice. Serve on a portion of sorghum, topped with cilantro, and alongside greens.

YIELD: 4 to 6 servings

Recipe Notes

• Can't or won't use sorghum? It can be replaced with brown rice, wheat berries, kamut, or pretty much any grain you fancy. If you need the dish to be gluten free, be mindful of the substitute you choose. Remember to adjust the cooking method and time accordingly.

• For a lower-fat version, use 1 cup (235 ml) full-fat coconut milk and ¾ cup (180 ml) water instead of the full can.

Quinoa and Veggies Stir-Fry

▶ **GRAIN**: QUINOA ▶ QUICK AND EASY ▶ GLUTEN-FREE POTENTIAL

Rice is nice, but how about a complete protein in the form of quinoa for a change, instead? This straightforward, scrumptious version gets our (and the testers') vote. Note that the quinoa absolutely needs to be cooked ahead and chilled in order to avoid mushy results.

1 tablespoon (15 ml) peanut, coconut, or other oil

2 small carrots, trimmed, peeled, and minced

¼ cup plus 2½ tablespoons (65 g) minced shallot

2½ cups (227 g) chopped green cabbage

1 small bell pepper (any color), seeded and diced

1½ tablespoons (15 g) minced garlic

2 tablespoons (30 ml) tamari, divided

1¾ cups (324 g) cooked and chilled quinoa

2 teaspoons to 1 tablespoon (10 to 15 ml) toasted sesame oil, as needed

1 cup (134 g) frozen green peas, thawed

Red pepper flakes or sriracha, to taste

GARNISHES:

White and green parts of scallion cut diagonally, toasted sesame seeds, pickled daikon radish, pickled ginger, chopped dry roasted peanuts or cashews, ume plum vinegar, to taste, for garnish

Place the oil, carrots, and shallot in a wok or large skillet. Sauté on medium-high heat until just softened, about 4 minutes, stirring occasionally. Add 1 tablespoon (15 ml) tamari, cabbage and bell pepper, and cook until slightly tender yet still crisp, about 4 minutes, stirring occasionally. Drizzle sesame oil as needed over the quinoa, and fold to lightly coat. Add the quinoa to the wok, remaining 1 tablespoon (15 ml) tamari, and peas. Sauté for another 2 minutes, stirring occasionally, until heated through and fragrant.

Remove from the heat, add red pepper flakes or sriracha. Choose one or more garnishes to taste. Serve immediately as is or alongside your favorite recipes of Asian-style seitan, tofu, tempeh, or beans.

YIELD: 4 servings

Kasha Varnishkes

▶ **GRAIN**: BUCKWHEAT ▶ SOY-FREE POTENTIAL

This hearty, comfort food dish is part of the Jewish tradition. While we won't claim that ours is authentic, it's still become a favorite. Kasha is the name given to buckwheat groats when they have been toasted. Farfalle pasta is sometimes referred to as bowtie pasta. But in fact, "farfalle" means butterflies. Call it what you will, this is stick-to-your-ribs happy food.

2 tablespoons (30 ml) olive oil, divided

¾ cup (120 g) chopped onion

1½ cups (5 ounces, or 140 g) sliced cremini mushrooms

½ cup (92 g) buckwheat, toasted (see Recipe Note)

2 tablespoons (30 ml) dry white wine, or additional broth

2 large cloves garlic, minced

1½ cups (355 ml) boiling water

1 tablespoon (18 g) vegan bouillon paste

1 teaspoon poultry seasoning blend

4 ounces (113 g) dry farfalle pasta (whole-grain or white), cooked and drained

5 ounces (140 g) baby spinach

Salt and pepper

Minced fresh dill, for garnish

Heat 1 tablespoon (15 ml) oil in a large skillet over medium heat. Cook the onions for 6 to 8 minutes, stirring occasionally, until tender and golden. Transfer to a plate and set aside. Add the mushrooms to the same skillet and cook until tender, 3 to 4 minutes. Transfer to the same plate as the onions, but do not mix the two. Add the remaining tablespoon (15 ml) olive oil to the skillet and add the buckwheat. Cook, stirring occasionally, until the buckwheat is covered with oil. Add the onions, wine, and garlic to the skillet. Cook until the wine is mostly absorbed.

Combine the boiling water, the bouillon paste, and the seasoning blend. Pour 1 cup (235 ml) of the broth into the skillet and cook for 20 to 30 minutes, stirring occasionally. Cook until the buckwheat is tender. Add the mushrooms, pasta, spinach, and splashes of the remaining broth until the spinach wilts and the mixture is hot throughout. Season to taste with salt and pepper. Garnish with the dill when serving.

YIELD: 4 generous servings

Recipe Note

If kasha (toasted buckwheat groats) is available, omit the toasting step. To toast buckwheat, heat a large skillet over medium heat. Add the buckwheat and cook until browned, stirring often.

SUPER SIDE IT WITH GRAINS!

Because whole grains give the best complements.

Making an incredible meal is easy when you're armed with the tastiest side dishes. Think of these recipes as light meals, too, depending on your appetite. Or combine two—or more—for a colorful culinary adventure on your plate!

Teff and Pea Fritters

▶ GRAIN: TEFF ▶ SOY-FREE POTENTIAL

We like to cook teff so that the texture of the grain is still somewhat present—like in these cute fritters that are crispy outside and tender inside. If your spice blend is a bit on the hot side, use slightly less. You can always boost the flavor with an extra pinch once cooked.

½ cup (100 g) dry teff

1 cup plus 6 tablespoons (325 ml) water, divided

2½ teaspoons (13 ml) fresh lemon juice

1 teaspoon grapeseed or olive oil

2½ tablespoons (15 g) minced scallion

1 large clove garlic, grated or pressed

2 tablespoons (4 g) packed minced fresh mint

1⅛ teaspoons ras el hanout (see page 53) or berbere spice (see page 16), plus extra for sprinkling

1 teaspoon Broth Powder (page 167)

⅜ teaspoon coarse kosher salt, to taste

¼ cup (34 g) frozen peas, thawed and drained

6 tablespoons (45 g) chickpea flour

1 tablespoon (8 g) whole-wheat pastry flour (or gluten-free flour blend to give these gluten-free potential)

High heat neutral-flavored oil, as needed

Combine teff with 1 cup (235 ml) water in a saucepan. Bring to a boil, cover with a lid, and lower the heat. Simmer until the liquid is absorbed, about 10 minutes. You're looking for a pilaflike texture, thus the lower grain-to-water ratio. Set aside to cool slightly.

In a large bowl, stir to combine the cooked teff with lemon juice, oil, scallion, garlic, mint, spice blend, broth powder, salt, and gently fold the peas into the mixture. In a separate small bowl, whisk to combine the remaining 6 tablespoons (90 ml) water with the chickpea flour. Make sure there are no lumps. Gently fold the chickpea mixture and whole-wheat flour into the teff mixture. Do not taste at this point; chickpea flour is bitter when uncooked. Refrigerate for 1 hour before use.

Shape the fritters using 1 packed tablespoon (22 g) of mixture and flattening into a disk of about 2 inches (5 cm) in diameter. Place on a piece of parchment paper while you shape the rest. You should get approximately 22 fritters in all. In a large skillet, heat a very thin layer of oil on medium-high heat. Lower the heat to medium, and cook the fritters in batches, about 3 minutes per side or until browned and crisp. Sprinkle each fritter with a tiny pinch of ras el hanout or berbere spice. Serve immediately with salad or vegetable of choice.

YIELD: 22 fritters

Fabulous Freekeh Patties
with Five-Star Sauce

▶ GRAIN: CRACKED FREEKEH

Burgers are a go-to in Tami's house, and these have been voted the best of the best. We always keep them in the freezer for ultrafast meals. We like to serve them with all the traditional burger fixings—don't forget the pickles! Some of our testers thought they should be served as steaks, perhaps with a sauce (see opposite page). They are that good!

FOR THE BURGERS:

2 cups (288 g) vital wheat gluten

1 cup (231 g) cooked cracked freekeh

1 tablespoon plus 1 teaspoon (10 g) garlic powder

1 tablespoon plus 1 teaspoon (10 g) onion powder

1 teaspoon ground cumin

1 teaspoon paprika

½ teaspoon ground black pepper

1 cup (235 ml) vegetable broth

2 tablespoons (30 ml) tamari

2 tablespoons (33 g) organic ketchup

1 tablespoon (15 ml) olive oil

1 teaspoon liquid smoke

Neutral-flavored oil, for cooking

FOR THE COOKING BROTH:

3 cups (705 ml) vegetable broth

1 tablespoon (15 ml) tamari

1 tablespoon (16 g) organic ketchup

½ teaspoon liquid smoke

Salt and black pepper

Preheat the oven to 300°F (150°C, or gas mark 2).

Stir together the vital wheat gluten, freekeh, garlic powder, onion powder, cumin, paprika, and black pepper in a medium-size bowl. Stir together the broth, tamari, ketchup, olive oil, and liquid smoke in a measuring cup. Combine the wet ingredients into the dry ingredients and stir. Add an additional tablespoon of broth (15 ml) or vital wheat gluten (9 g), if needed, to form a cohesive dough. Knead for a few minutes, then divide into 8 equal portions, about 3.7 ounces (105 g) each. Using your hands and a Silpat, pat the burgers out to about 3 inches (7.5 cm) across, and ½-inch (1.3 cm) thick. You may need to pinch parts of the burger together to "patch" them.

Heat a thin layer of neutral-flavored oil in large skillet over medium-high heat. Cook the burgers in batches for 3 to 5 minutes until browned. Turn and cook the second side for 3 to 4 minutes until browned.

Stir together the cooking-broth ingredients in a large roasting pan. Put the burgers into the broth. Cover the pan tightly with foil and bake for 1 hour. Turn off the heat and leave the burgers in the oven for 1 hour longer. Let cool in any remaining broth. The burgers can be wrapped airtight and frozen for up to 3 months or refrigerated for up to 3 days. Burgers should be cooled completely before serving for the best texture and, if frozen, should be thawed.

Heat a thin layer of oil in a large skillet over medium-high heat. Cook for 3 to 6 minutes until browned and crisp. Turn over to cook the second side, then serve on buns with toppings of choice.

YIELD: 8 burgers

Five-Star Sauce

When our testers were reviewing the patties, some thought that they were *too good* to be served as burgers—and that led Tami to feature them with this delectable sauce. Yes, I just said delectable. Upon first taste, Jim declared it to be "five star!" To dress up the patties a bit more (after all, we made a sauce *just* for them) we dredged them in seasoned flour (about 1 tablespoon [8 g] per 2 patties) before panfrying as usual.

1 large shallot, (about 2.5 ounces, or 70 g), peeled, chopped into 1-inch (2.5 cm) pieces

2 cloves garlic, peeled, sliced lengthwise

2 tablespoons (30 ml) olive oil

Salt and pepper

1¾ cups (415 ml) vegetable broth, divided

¼ teaspoon dried berbere, more to taste

¼ teaspoon dried thyme, crumbled

2 tablespoons (16 g) cornstarch

2 teaspoons (10 ml) ume plum vinegar

Preheat the oven to 400°F (200°C, or gas mark 6).

Combine the shallot, garlic, and olive oil in a small baking dish. Stir to coat the vegetables, then season with salt and pepper. Bake for 18 to 20 minutes until just turning golden. Transfer to a blender and add 1½ cups (355 ml) broth. Process until smooth.

Heat a medium-size saucepan over medium-low heat. Toast the berbere for 4 to 6 minutes, stirring often, until fragrant. Add the blended broth mixture and the thyme. Bring to a boil over high heat, then reduce to simmer for 5 minutes. Whisk the cornstarch into the remaining ¼ cup (60 ml) broth. Then whisk the cornstarch/broth into the hot broth mixture. Continue to simmer and whisk until thickened, 3 to 5 minutes. Whisk in the vinegar, then season to taste with salt and pepper.

YIELD: 1¾ cups (415 ml)

BBQ Bulgur Burgers

▶ GRAIN: BULGUR

Even though these awesome wheat-based burgers aren't held together by vital wheat gluten, they still manage to come out sturdy and firm enough to be eaten on a bun. Hooray for bulgur and beans! Be picky with the barbecue sauce here, as it is the star of the show in this recipe—aside from bulgur and beans, of course.

½ cup (80 g) dry quick-cooking bulgur wheat

1 cup (235 ml) vegetable broth

1 can (15 ounces, or 425 g) chickpeas, drained and rinsed

½ cup (120 ml) favorite vegan barbecue sauce, plus extra for serving

2 tablespoons (15 g) nutritional yeast

½ teaspoon ground cumin

½ teaspoon smoked or regular paprika

½ cup (80 g) minced red onion

2 tablespoons (20 g) minced garlic

½ cup (40 g) whole-wheat or regular panko bread crumbs

Nonstick cooking spray or oil spray, for baking

Place the bulgur in a rice cooker or medium pot. Cover with broth and stir to combine. Follow the manufacturer's instructions if using a rice cooker. Bring to a boil if cooking on the stove. Cover with a lid, lower the temperature, and simmer until tender, 12 to 15 minutes. Remove from the heat and let stand 5 minutes still covered, then fluff and let cool before use.

Place the chickpeas, barbecue sauce, nutritional yeast, cumin, paprika, onion, and garlic in a food processor. Pulse to break the chickpeas: You're not looking for a paste, but there should be no whole chickpea left. Remove approximately half of this mixture and place in a large bowl. Set aside. Add the panko to the food processor. Process until a paste forms. Transfer this mixture and the bulgur to the large bowl, and thoroughly combine. Divide into 8 equal portions of approximately ⅓ cup (100 g), or for smaller burgers, 10 portions of ¼ cup (80 g). Shape into patties of a generous 3 inches (8 cm) in diameter. Place on a large baking sheet lined with parchment paper. Cover with plastic wrap. Store in the refrigerator for at least 30 minutes, or overnight.

Preheat the oven to 375°F (190°C, or gas mark 5). Remove the plastic wrap. Lightly coat each burger with cooking spray and bake for 20 minutes. Carefully flip, and bake for another 10 minutes or until firm. Let stand 5 minutes before serving with extra barbecue sauce.

YIELD: 8 to 10 burgers

Super-Quick Quinoa and Black Bean Sliders

▶ GRAIN: QUINOA ▶ SOY-FREE POTENTIAL ▶ QUICK AND EASY

Leftovers never tasted better than they do in these sliders. Just because we call them sliders, don't let that limit your imagination. They are wonderful on salads or eaten like fritters with salsa for dipping. Be sure to brown them well to make them addictively crispy on the outside.

1 cup (172 g) prepared black beans

2 cups (340 g) Corn-oa (page 116)

2 tablespoons (30 ml) prepared barbecue sauce

⅓ cup (38 g) all-purpose flour, more if needed

Neutral-flavored oil, for cooking

Buns, lettuce, tomato slices, bell pepper rings, pickles, other condiments of choice

Put the black beans in a medium-size bowl. With your hands (or a potato masher) mash the beans until mostly pasty. Some of the beans are fine if left whole. Stir in the Corn-oa and barbecue sauce until combined. Add the flour and stir well. Using a ¼ cup (60 ml) measure, scoop a measuring cup of the mixture. Pat and press it into a patty about ½-inch (1.3 cm) thick. The mixture should hold together firmly. If not, return the mixture to the bowl and add an additional tablespoon (8 g) flour and mix again.

Heat a thin layer of oil in a large skillet over medium-high heat. Cook the sliders in batches until browned and crisp, 4 to 5 minutes. Turn them over to cook the second side for 3 to 5 minutes or until browned and crisp.

YIELD: 8 sliders

Pepper Grain Sausages

▶ **GRAIN**: TRITICALE BERRIES ▶ SOY-FREE POTENTIAL

You must have a taste of these outstanding sausages in Einkorn Paella (page 41) or Muhammara Redux with Sorghum (page 71)! They're also great eaten as a snack, in salads, or even sandwiches. Be sure to grill or brown them to bring out the full flavor and elevate the texture of the sausages. If you cannot find triticale berries, use the same weight of cooked spelt berries, kamut, or wheat berries.

1 heaping cup (190 g) cooked triticale berries

Scant 6 ounces (1 generous cup, or 165 g) fire-roasted bell pepper

¼ cup (30 g) nutritional yeast

2 tablespoons (32 g) tahini paste

2 tablespoons (30 ml) fresh lemon juice

½ cup (120 ml) water, divided

2 teaspoons (10 ml) grapeseed or olive oil

2 teaspoons (5 g) ground cumin

2 teaspoons (5 g) Broth Powder (page 167)

2 teaspoons (6 g) garlic powder

2 teaspoons (5 g) onion powder

2 teaspoons (4 g) smoked paprika

1 generous teaspoon coarse kosher salt

1 cup (144 g) vital wheat gluten

Place triticale berries, peppers, nutritional yeast, tahini, lemon juice, ¼ cup (60 ml) water, oil, cumin, broth, garlic and onion powders, paprika, and salt in a food processor. Process until partially smooth: It's okay if the grains are still visible. Transfer to a large bowl and add the gluten on top. Stir with a spoon, then switch to stirring with one hand, making sure to squeeze the mixture to thoroughly combine. Add an extra 1 tablespoon (15 ml) water or (8 g) gluten, if needed, to make a soft, workable dough.

Divide the mixture evenly (about 3 ounces, or 90 g each) between eight 12-inch (30.5 cm) pieces of foil. Form into sausages of about 7 inches (18 cm) long. Roll the foil tightly around the mixture, twisting the ends to enclose the sausages. Prepare a steamer. Cover and steam the sausages for 1 hour 15 minutes. Remove foil (careful of the steam) and let cool on a wire rack.

The sausages taste best when they spend a whole night in the refrigerator before serving. They must be cooked until slightly browned. Cook on the grill or in a (lightly greased or dry) pan on medium-low heat for approximately 10 minutes, making sure to roll the sausage to brown all over. Store tightly wrapped in the refrigerator for up to 1 week or freeze for up to 2 months.

YIELD: 8 sausages (7 inches, or 18 cm)

Cracked Wheat Koftas

▶ **GRAIN**: CRACKED WHEAT ▶ SOY-FREE POTENTIAL

We love finger foods, and these slightly yellow-hued, spicy wheatballs have an awesome texture that no one can resist! Make a quick dipping sauce by thoroughly combining ½ cup (120 g) Basic Cashew Cream (page 166) or unsweetened plain vegan yogurt with 1 tablespoon (30 g) of your favorite vegan chutney.

1 cup (160 g) dry cracked wheat

3 cups (705 ml) vegetable broth

1 cup plus 3 tablespoons (130 g) finely grated carrot (about 2)

5 tablespoons (50 g) minced shallot

Generous 1½ tablespoons (15 g) minced garlic

1 teaspoon garam masala

1 teaspoon packed and slightly heaping grated fresh ginger

1 teaspoon dried cilantro or 2 tablespoons (2 g) minced fresh cilantro leaves

½ teaspoon ground coriander

½ teaspoon turmeric

⅛ to ¼ teaspoon cayenne pepper, to taste

½ teaspoon fine sea salt

1 tablespoon (15 ml) fresh lemon juice

1 tablespoon (15 ml) grapeseed or olive oil

¼ cup (30 g) chickpea flour

Nonstick cooking spray or oil spray

Place the cracked wheat and broth in a rice cooker or large pot. Stir to combine. Follow the manufacturer's instructions if using a rice cooker. Bring to a boil if cooking on the stove. Cover with a lid, lower the temperature, and simmer until the grain is tender, about 15 minutes. Drain, if needed, and let cool to room temperature before use.

In a large bowl, stir to combine the cooled wheat, carrot, shallot, garlic, garam masala, ginger, cilantro, coriander, turmeric, cayenne pepper, salt, lemon juice, and oil. Sprinkle the flour on top. Stir with a spoon at first, switching to using one hand to thoroughly combine. Lightly coat 30 cups out of two mini muffin tins with cooking spray. Grab 1 packed tablespoon (25 g) of mixture, roll into a ball between the palms of your hands, and place in the prepared tins. Refrigerate uncovered for 1 hour.

Preheat the oven to 375°F (190°C, or gas mark 5). Lightly coat the top of the koftas with cooking spray before baking for 25 minutes. Gently flip the slightly fragile koftas. Bake for another 5 minutes. Let stand 10 minutes before serving.

YIELD: 30 koftas

Italian Wheatballs

▶ **GRAIN**: BULGUR

Years ago, Tami's friend, Lisa Coulson (a.k.a. Panda with Cookie), wrote a zine filled with ballz recipes. With a handful of variations, this recipe is a mini homage to her. Thanks, Lisa, for the tasty inspiration. The bulgur-and-gluten combo forms a solid base for the wheatballs. Try these versions, at right, or create your own. Go wild!

1 cup (200 g) bulgur (Bob's Red Mill or Arrowhead Mills)

1 cup (144 g) vital wheat gluten

½ cup (80 g) very finely minced onion

2 teaspoons (3 g) Italian seasoning blend

2 teaspoons (5 g) garlic powder

¼ teaspoon red pepper flakes

⅔ cup (160 ml) vegetable broth

2 tablespoons (33 g) organic ketchup

1 tablespoon (15 ml) tamari

½ teaspoon fine sea salt

¼ teaspoon ground black pepper

Olive oil cooking spray

Preheat the oven to 375°F (190°C, or gas mark 5). Lightly oil a baking sheet with the olive oil cooking spray, or use a Silpat.

Combine the bulgur through the red pepper flakes in a medium-size bowl. Combine the remaining ingredients in a measuring cup. Pour the wet ingredients into the dry and knead a few minutes. The mixture should be cohesive and hold together. Scoop 1 tablespoon (23 g) of the mixture and shape into a ball. Place the ball on the prepared baking sheet. Continue until all of the mixture is formed into 20 to 24 balls. Bake for 20 minutes. Turn over to bake 20 minutes longer, then reduce the heat to 300°F (150 °C, or gas mark 2) and bake for 15 minutes. Up to this point, the wheatballs may be made ahead and refrigerated airtight for 2 days or frozen for 2 months.

For serving, the wheatballs must be cooked in liquid. For spaghetti sauce with wheatballs, bring your favorite sauce to a simmer. Add the balls and simmer for 30 minutes, stirring gently and occasionally. The wheatballs may also be cooked in broth in the same manner, drained, and used as desired. Try them as an appetizer on toothpicks with marinara sauce for dipping.

YIELD: 20 to 24 wheatballs

VARIATIONS

Mexican version:

Omit the Italian seasoning and red pepper flakes. Add 2 teaspoons (5 g) ground cumin, ½ teaspoon cayenne pepper. Cook as above in broth, or add to the Albóndigas Soup (page 137) after baking.

Indian version:

Omit the Italian seasoning and red pepper flakes. Add 2 teaspoons (4 g) curry powder (mild or hot), 1 teaspoon ground cumin, ½ teaspoon ground coriander, ½ teaspoon garam masala, ½ teaspoon ground ginger. After simmering in broth, serve in a curry sauce. Or try the Sort-of-Like-a-Samosa Soup (page 133).

Asian version:

Omit the Italian seasoning and red pepper flakes. Add 1 teaspoon five-spice powder, ½ teaspoon Szechuan seasoning, ½ teaspoon ground ginger, ½ teaspoon sesame seeds (optional). After simmering, drain, and serve with sweet-and-sour sauce or a Korean-style barbecue sauce.

Moroccan version:

Omit the Italian seasoning and red pepper flakes. Add 1 teaspoon ground cumin, 1 teaspoon ground coriander, 1 teaspoon paprika, ½ teaspoon garlic powder, and ¼ teaspoon ground cinnamon.

For consistently sized wheatballs, use a 1-inch (2.5 cm) melon baller.

For smaller wheatballs, use 1½ teaspoons of the mixture and bake for half the time.

Zhoug Farro Falafel

▶ GRAIN: FARRO ▶ SOY-FREE POTENTIAL

Zhoug is a Yemeni spicy herb paste made with hot peppers, fresh herbs, cumin, and more. It works so well combined with these falafel ingredients! If you fear heat, switch to using only 1 small jalapeño pepper (0.9 ounce, or 25 g) instead. See the Recipe Note for a dip suggestion.

1 cup (165 g) cooked farro or (194 g) spelt berries

1 cup (164 g) cooked chickpeas

2 small jalapeño peppers (1.75 ounces, or 50 g), trimmed and seeded

¼ cup (6 g) packed fresh cilantro leaves

¼ cup (15 g) packed fresh flat-leaf parsley

1 tablespoon (10 g) minced garlic

½ teaspoon coarse kosher salt

½ teaspoon ground cumin

¼ teaspoon ground black pepper, to taste

⅛ teaspoon ground cardamom or ¼ teaspoon ground allspice

2 tablespoons (30 ml) grapeseed or olive oil

1 tablespoon (15 ml) fresh lemon juice

¼ cup (40 g) minced red onion or (20 g) scallion

6 tablespoons (45 g) chickpea flour

¼ teaspoon baking powder

Nonstick cooking spray or oil spray

In a food processor, place the farro and chickpeas. Process until the mixture is partially smooth: It's okay to have chunky pieces of beans, but none should remain whole. Transfer to a medium bowl.

To the food processor, add the peppers, cilantro, parsley, garlic, salt, cumin, black pepper, cardamom, oil, and lemon juice. Process until smooth, stopping to scrape the sides with a rubber spatula, if needed. Transfer to the same bowl and stir to combine. Sprinkle the flour and baking powder on top, folding gently to thoroughly combine. Cover with a lid, and refrigerate for 1 hour, up to overnight.

Preheat the oven to 375°F (190°C, or gas mark 5). Lightly coat a mini muffin tin with cooking spray. Grab 1 packed, slightly heaping tablespoon (24 g) of mixture, and place in the prepared tin. Bake for 15 minutes. Gently flip with a small baker's spatula and press down slightly with spatula. Bake for another 10 to 15 minutes until firm and golden brown. Let stand 10 minutes before serving.

YIELD: 20 to 24 falafel

Recipe Note

For a simple dipping sauce: Whisk to combine ¾ cup (180 g) unsweetened plain vegan yogurt or Basic Cashew Cream (page 166), 1½ tablespoons (6 g) minced fresh parsley, cilantro, or mint, 1½ table-spoons (23 ml) lemon juice, 1½ tablespoons (24 g) tahini paste, 1 to 2 cloves garlic, grated or pressed, and salt and pepper to taste. Yields approximately ¾ cup (200 g) dipping sauce.

Millet Amaranth Croquettes

▶ GRAINS: MILLET AND AMARANTH

We've kept the flavor of these tasty croquettes neutral enough so that they can be combined with any favorite vegan dipping sauce. Check out the recipe directions for serving suggestions.

½ cup (110 g) dry millet, rinsed and drained

¼ cup (45 g) dry amaranth

1½ cups (355 ml) vegetable broth

½ fire-roasted bell pepper (2 ounces, or 56 g), minced, drained, and patted dry

4 cloves garlic, grated

2 tablespoons (30 ml) fresh lemon juice

2 tablespoons (32 g) tahini paste

2 tablespoons (15 g) nutritional yeast

2 tablespoons (36 g) light miso

2 tablespoons (24 g) potato starch or (16 g) organic cornstarch

¼ teaspoon fine sea salt

2 tablespoons (7 g) minced parsley

¼ cup (30 g) whole-wheat pastry flour, plus extra if needed, or gluten-free flour mix

Nonstick cooking spray or oil spray

Place the millet and amaranth in a rice cooker or large pot. Cover with broth, stir to combine. Follow the manufacturer's instructions if using a rice cooker. Bring to a boil if cooking on the stove. Cover with a lid, lower the temperature, and simmer until the liquid is absorbed, about 15 minutes.

In the meantime, mix the remaining ingredients (except flour) in a large bowl, then add the millet and amaranth, stirring to thoroughly combine. Cover loosely and chill in the refrigerator at least 2 hours up to overnight.

Preheat the oven to 375°F (190°C, or gas mark 5). Stir the flour into the mixture. Note that it will be moist. However, if it's more liquid than moist, add up to ¼ cup (60 g) extra flour, 1 tablespoon (8 g) at a time until it becomes more manageable. Coat a mini muffin tin with cooking spray. Scoop 1 packed, barely heaping tablespoon (30 g) of the mix, and drop into the tin. You should get 24 croquettes in all. Lightly coat the tops with cooking spray and gently even out the tops with your fingers. Bake for 20 minutes and gently flip with a small spatula. Bake for another 10 minutes or until golden brown but not dry. Let stand 10 minutes before serving with your favorite vegan marinara, barbecue sauce, or other dipping sauce. Leftover Slightly Cheesy Cashew Sauce (page 166), it would be perfect as well.

YIELD: 24 croquettes

Cajun Buckwheat Rice Fries

▶ **GRAIN**: BUCKWHEAT GROATS ▶ GLUTEN-FREE POTENTIAL ▶ SOY-FREE POTENTIAL

These crispy fries beg to be dipped in flavored ketchup! For one person, combine 3 tablespoons (51 g) organic ketchup, hot sauce to taste, and a few pinches of Cajun seasoning, if desired. If you cannot locate brown rice farina, you can make your own using a hand grain grinder or coffee grinder. You could also use whole-wheat farina (won't have gluten-free potential in this case) or millet farina in its place.

½ cup (90 g) dry buckwheat groats

½ cup (82 g) brown rice farina

1 tablespoon (8 g) nutritional yeast

1½ tablespoons (12 g) Broth Powder (page 167)

1 teaspoon onion powder

Generous ½ teaspoon garlic powder

½ teaspoon fine sea salt

2 cups (470 ml) water

Nonstick cooking spray or oil spray

Place buckwheat in 4 batches of 2 tablespoons (23 g) in coffee grinder or miniblender, pulsing to break down into small bits but not flour (about 6 short-burst grinds). Transfer to a medium pot. Add the farina, nutritional yeast, broth powder, Cajun seasoning, onion and garlic powders, and salt. Whisk with water. Bring to a gentle boil on medium-high heat, whisking constantly. Lower the heat to a low simmer and cook 2 minutes, whisking constantly. Cover and cook for 6 minutes, removing the lid occasionally to stir. Adjust the heat, if needed, to prevent scorching. When the mixture is too thick for whisking, switch to a rubber spatula. Remove the lid, and keep cooking until very thick (like dry mashed potatoes), about 4 minutes.

Spread evenly in an 8-inch (20 cm) square baking pan coated with cooking spray, using an angled spatula. Do not cover the pan. Cool at room temperature. Cover with plastic wrap and chill for at least 2 hours or overnight.

Preheat the oven to 425°F (220°C, or gas mark 7). Lightly grease a large-rimmed baking sheet with cooking spray. Remove from pan, cut into four 4-inch (10 cm) squares. Cut each square into 5 or 6 fries, for a total of 20 to 24 fries.

Lightly coat with cooking spray, and space evenly on prepared sheet. Bake for 15 minutes and flip. Bake for another 10 to 15 minutes or until browned and crisp. Serve with flavored or plain ketchup.

YIELD: 4 servings

Tacu Tacu

▶ **GRAIN**: BROWN RICE ▶ GLUTEN-FREE POTENTIAL ▶ SOY-FREE POTENTIAL
▶ QUICK AND EASY

Tacu tacu, or bean and rice fritters, are a Peruvian mainstay. They were initially brought to Peru by way of the African slaves. With the crispy outside and almost creamy inside, it's easy to see why the dish quickly rose in popularity. Plus, who can resist saying it? Tami first heard about it from her Peruvian friend, Monica, to whom she says *gracias*!

½ cup (120 g) prepared salsa (spicy is good here!)

½ cup (120 ml) water, plus enough to make 1¾ cups (415 ml) liquid (or according to package)

1 cup (180 g) dry short-grain brown rice

2 tablespoons (30 ml) olive oil, divided

½ cup (80 g) finely minced onion

1 can (15 ounces, or 425 g) butter beans, drained

2 cloves garlic, minced

2 teaspoons (5 g) ground cumin

½ teaspoon smoked paprika

½ teaspoon fine sea salt

⅓ cup (80 ml) vegetable broth

Black pepper

Blend the salsa with ½ cup (120 ml) of water until smooth. Add enough water for a total of 1¾ cups (415 ml) of liquid, or the amount the rice package requires for 1 cup (180 g) of dry rice. Cook according to package directions and let cool.

Heat 1 tablespoon (15 ml) of oil in a large skillet over medium heat. Add the onion, beans, garlic, cumin, paprika, salt, and broth. Cook, while smashing the beans, to create a refried bean consistency. This should take 5 to 7 minutes. Season to taste with pepper. Remove from the heat and stir in the rice. Once cool enough to handle, the mixture should be shapeable. Using ½ cup (5 ounces, 140 g) of the mixture, form into a football-shaped pancake that is a generous 1-inch (2.5 cm) thick.

Heat the remaining tablespoon (15 ml) of olive oil in a large, nonstick skillet over medium-high heat. Cook the mixture, continuing to shape and pack it with a metal spatula until browned, 4 to 6 minutes. Turn over to cook the second side until browned, 3 to 5 minutes. Serve hot.

YIELD: 6 servings

Aztec Tofu

▶ GRAIN: AMARANTH ▶ GLUTEN-FREE POTENTIAL

The crispy coating gives way to a slightly spicy full-flavor tofu that is a refreshing change of pace from most everyday tofu recipes. We like to serve it with the Corn-oa (page 116), but it pairs well with rice, too. Heads up! This tofu is best marinated for at least 24 hours, so plan ahead.

FOR THE TOFU AND MARINADE:

1 pound (454 g) extra-firm tofu, drained and pressed, cut into ¼-inch (6 mm) slices

¼ cup (60 ml) vegetable broth

¼ cup (60 ml) dry red wine, or additional broth

1 tablespoon (15 ml) tamari

1 teaspoon chili powder

1 teaspoon ground cumin

1 teaspoon garlic powder

1 teaspoon onion powder

½ teaspoon fine sea salt

FOR THE BREADING AND COOKING:

¾ cup (180 ml) plain, unsweetened vegan milk

⅓ cup plus 1 tablespoon (71 g) amaranth

2 tablespoons (33 g) organic ketchup

1 teaspoon chili powder

1 cup (160 g) corn flour, (not cornmeal) divided

Salt and pepper

Neutral-flavored oil, for cooking

To make the tofu and marinade: Whisk the broth, tamari, and seasonings together in a 9 x 13-inch (23 cm x 33 cm) pan. Put the tofu in the marinade and turn to coat. Cover with plastic wrap and refrigerate for 24 hours or up to 3 days.

To make the breading: Whisk the milk, amaranth, ketchup, and chili powder together in a shallow dish. Whisk in ¾ cup (120 g) of the corn flour. Season with salt and pepper. Put the remaining corn flour on a plate.

Heat a thin layer of oil in a large skillet over medium-high heat. Dredge the tofu in the corn flour, then in the batter. Place the tofu in the skillet. The batter will slightly spread from the tofu. Cook for 3 to 5 minutes until the batter that has spread is browned. Gently turn the tofu over. Turning the tofu over too soon will cause the breading to stick to the pan, not the tofu. Cook the tofu on the second side until browned, 3 to 5 minutes. Cook the remaining tofu in batches, if necessary.

YIELD: 4 to 6 servings

Cajun Rice Patties

▶ **GRAIN:** SWEET BROWN RICE ▶ SOY-FREE POTENTIAL

These crispy rice patties are even more delightful drizzled with hot sauce or sprinkled with extra Cajun seasoning. Serve with a lightly dressed crisp lettuce or sliced, summery, heirloom tomatoes.

½ cup (98 g) dry sweet brown rice, rinsed and drained

2 cups (470 ml) vegetable broth

3 tablespoons (18 g) minced scallion

2 cloves garlic, minced

1½ teaspoons Cajun seasoning (choose a salt-free blend, such as Frontier), plus extra for garnish

1¼ teaspoons fresh thyme leaves, minced

Generous ½ teaspoon coarse kosher salt, to taste

½ to 1 teaspoon hot sauce (such as Frank's), to taste

½ teaspoon mild Dijon mustard

⅓ cup (65 g) cooked white beans (choose moist beans), mashed

¾ cup (60 g) vegan panko bread crumbs, as needed

High heat neutral-flavored oil, as needed

Lemon wedges, to serve

Combine the rice and broth in a pot. Bring to a boil, lower the heat, and cover with a lid. Simmer until tender, about 30 to 35 minutes. Drain if needed. Set aside to cool slightly.

Transfer the rice to a large bowl and stir the scallion, garlic, Cajun seasoning, thyme, salt, hot sauce, and mustard to combine. Add the beans and thoroughly stir to combine. Add ½ cup (40 g) of bread crumbs to begin with. The total amount needed will depend on how moist the beans are. The mixture should be quite thick and just moist enough without being sticky or too dry. Cover and place in the refrigerator for 1 hour.

Have a piece of parchment paper handy or shape the patties as you go. Use ¼ cup (57 g) of mixture per patty and shape into generous 3-inch (8 cm) disks. Place on the parchment.

Heat a thin layer of oil in a large skillet. Cook the patties in batches on medium heat, 6 minutes per side or until golden brown and crispy. You want to cook them long enough so that they get a crispy coating and not-too-moist inside. Adjust the heat as needed. Serve with wedges of lemon.

YIELD: 6 to 8 patties

Recipe Note

You can make your own Cajun seasoning by combining ½ teaspoon paprika, ¼ teaspoon garlic powder, ¼ teaspoon onion powder, ¼ teaspoon dried marjoram or oregano, ⅛ teaspoon cayenne pepper (to taste), and ⅛ teaspoon ground cumin. This will yield just the right amount for this recipe.

Quinoa and Beer Onion Rings

▶ **GRAIN**: QUINOA ▶ SOY-FREE POTENTIAL ▶ QUICK AND EASY

These onion rings are both elegant and casual. Imagine two of these atop a seitan steak in a fancy restaurant. And just think: What if you could get these at your local dive bar? This combo makes them perfect any time.

1 cup (185 g) cooked quinoa
(We like tri-color, but any is fine)

½ cup plus 2 tablespoons (75 g)
all-purpose flour (see Recipe Note)

1 teaspoon cornstarch

¾ teaspoon fine sea salt

½ teaspoon garlic powder

¼ teaspoon dried parsley

¼ teaspoon ground black pepper

¾ cup (180 ml) vegan lager or light ale

1 medium onion, sliced into ½-inch
(1.3 cm) thick rings

High heat neutral-flavored oil,
for cooking

Line a baking sheet with a brown bag.

Combine the quinoa, flour, cornstarch, salt, garlic powder, parsley, and black pepper in a pie plate. Stir to combine with a fork. Stir in the beer. The mixture will be thick and a little lumpy. Set aside

Heat approximately ½ inch (1.3 cm) of oil in a large skillet over medium to medium-high heat. Dip the onion rings into the batter. Coat them well, but allow any excess to drip off. Cooking in batches, put them in the skillet. Cook for 3 to 5 minutes until golden. Turn over and cook the second side for 3 to 5 minutes or until golden. Transfer to the paper bag to drain while cooking the remaining onion rings.

YIELD: 4 servings

> **Recipe Note**
> Sometimes the batter refuses to stick to the onions. If that's the case, dust them with some extra flour first.

Quinoa and Cornmeal–Crusted Fried Green Tomatoes

▶ **GRAIN**: CORNMEAL ▶ GLUTEN-FREE POTENTIAL ▶ SOY-FREE POTENTIAL

Beautifully crisp, these fried green tomatoes won't be like any you have ever had. We've carefully layered the flavor in each of the steps so that these pack a tasty punch.

FOR THE SALSA-SPIKED SAUCE:

¼ cup (35 g) cashews

½ cup (120 ml) water

½ cup (132 g) prepared salsa

1 tablespoon (15 ml) red wine vinegar

1 tablespoon (15 ml) plain, unsweetened vegan milk

1 chipotle pepper in adobo, optional

Salt and pepper

FOR THE TOMATOES AND SERVING:

½ cup (56 g) quinoa flour, divided

¼ cup (35 g) coarse cornmeal

½ teaspoon onion powder

Salt and pepper

½ cup (120 ml) plain, unsweetened vegan milk

1 teaspoon red wine vinegar

1 teaspoon hot sauce, optional

2 large green tomatoes, cut into ½-inch (1.3 cm) thick slices

2 cups (150 g) chopped cabbage

½ cup (82 g) frozen corn kernels, thawed under hot water

½ cup (86 g) cooked black beans

1 tablespoon (9 g) minced scallion

High heat neutral-flavored oil, for cooking

To make the sauce: Bring the cashews and water to a boil. Simmer for 15 minutes and drain. Transfer to a small high-powered blender and add the remaining sauce ingredients. Blend until smooth. Refrigerate until needed.

To make the tomatoes: For the dry ingredients, put ¼ cup (28 g) quinoa flour on two plates. Add the cornmeal and onion powder to one of the plates. Season both plates with salt and pepper.

Whisk the milk, vinegar, and hot sauce together. Set aside.

Heat ¼ inch (6 mm) of oil in a large skillet over medium-high heat. Working in batches, keeping one hand wet and one hand dry, dredge the tomatoes in the quinoa flour, then the milk mixture, then the cornmeal mixture. Pat to coat the tomatoes well. Cook them in the oil until the tomatoes start to look slightly brown on the bottom edges, 3 to 5 minutes. Gently turn with a fork, away from your body in case of spatters. Cook for 4 to 5 minutes until golden brown. Drain very briefly on a paper towel, if desired.

To serve, spread the cabbage on a platter. Top with the tomatoes and drizzle with the sauce, as desired. Sprinkle evenly with the corn, beans, and scallion. Serve immediately.

YIELD: 8 to 10 green tomato slices, ¾ cup sauce (180 ml)

Mexican Buckwheat and Corn Rounds

▶ **GRAINS**: BUCKWHEAT GROATS AND CORNMEAL ▶ GLUTEN-FREE POTENTIAL
▶ SOY-FREE POTENTIAL

Using a whoopie pie pan guarantees the best-shaped results for these savory whole-grain rounds. If not available, use 3-inch (7.6 cm) pie pans to shape and then transfer the rounds to a baking sheet lined with parchment paper. These can be served with the dressing from the Tex-Mex Freekeh Salad (page 156), but any salsa will do. If you love avocados and a drizzle of lime, they are nice complements, too!

Nonstick cooking spray or oil spray

½ cup (90 g) dry buckwheat groats

½ cup (86 g) organic medium cornmeal (such as Bob's Red Mill)

1½ teaspoons mild to medium chili powder

½ teaspoon ground cumin

½ teaspoon onion powder

½ teaspoon fine sea salt, to taste

¼ teaspoon dried oregano leaves

¼ teaspoon ground coriander

¼ teaspoon garlic powder

¼ teaspoon smoked or regular paprika

2 cups (470 ml) vegetable broth

½ cup (82 g) frozen corn kernels

¼ cup (75 g) vegan salsa (green or red)

Lightly coat a whoopie pie pan with cooking spray. Set aside.

Place groats in 4 batches in coffee grinder or mini blender, pulsing to break down into small bits but not flour (about 6 short-burst grinds). Transfer to a medium pot, with cornmeal, chili powder, cumin, onion, salt, oregano, coriander, garlic, and paprika. Whisk with broth, then add and whisk frozen corn and salsa. Bring to a gentle boil on medium-high heat, whisking occasionally. Reduce the heat to a low simmer, and cover with lid. Cook for 8 minutes, removing the lid occasionally to stir with a rubber spatula. Adjust the heat, if needed, to prevent scorching. Cook and stir another 2 minutes until the mixture is very thick.

Scoop out about 3 packed, slightly heaping tablespoons (65 g) of the mixture into each prepared hole: An ice cream or cookie scoop works well for this. Even out tops, and lightly coat the tops with cooking spray. Let cool at room temperature. Cover with plastic wrap and refrigerate for 2 hours or overnight.

Preheat the oven to 400°F (200°C, or gas mark 6). Remove the plastic wrap. Bake 20 minutes and carefully flip. Bake for another 10 minutes until golden brown. Let stand a few minutes before serving.

Alternatively, these can be panfried in batches in a thin layer of oil in a skillet, on medium-high heat for about 8 minutes on each side until golden brown. Adjust the heat, as needed.

YIELD: 12 3-inch (8 cm) rounds

Home-style Bulgur Gravy

▶ **GRAIN**: BULGUR ▶ QUICK AND EASY

This gorgeous gravy is sure to become your mashed potatoes' new bff. Try it on grilled seitan, too. The secret ingredient is teff flour. It brings loads of hearty flavor, especially when you consider the gravy can be made in minutes. One word of caution: It doesn't store well, so be prepared to eat it all!

2 tablespoons (30 ml) neutral-flavored oil

3 tablespoons (30 g) minced onion

2 tablespoons (16 g) minced carrot

2 tablespoons (30 g) minced celery

1 clove garlic, minced

1 cup (60 g) minced cremini mushrooms

½ cup (100 g) cooked bulgur

2 tablespoons (16 g) all-purpose flour

2 tablespoons (20 g) teff flour

½ teaspoon ground cumin

Pinch cayenne pepper

3 tablespoons (45 ml) dry white wine

1 cup (235 ml) vegetable broth

1 tablespoon (15 ml) tamari

½ teaspoon liquid smoke, or to taste

Salt and pepper

Heat the oil, onion, carrot, and celery in a large skillet over medium heat. Cook, stirring occasionally with a whisk, until the onion is fragrant, 3 to 4 minutes. Add the garlic, mushrooms, and bulgur. Cook for 2 minutes, then add the flours, cumin, and cayenne pepper. Cook, and whisk for 3 to 5 minutes to cook the flour. The mixture will be very clumpy and pasty.

Add the wine to deglaze the pan, whisking to combine the ingredients. Whisk in the broth. Add the tamari and liquid smoke. Continue to whisk and cook until thickened, 3 to 4 minutes. Season to taste with salt and pepper.

YIELD: 1⅔ cups (466 g)

Presto Pesto Spelt Bites

▶ **GRAIN**: SPELT ▶ SOY-FREE POTENTIAL ▶ QUICK AND EASY

These flavorful little bites are so easy to make, especially if you have pesto and cooked grain handy. They're sure to please the finger-food lovers of the household. Be sure to keep some of the pesto to make our Creamy Pesto Asparagus Einkorn (page 56)!

FOR THE PESTO:

2½ cups (60 g) fresh basil leaves

1½ cups (45 g) fresh baby spinach

1 tablespoon (8 g) Broth Powder (page 167)

1 tablespoon (15 ml) fresh lemon juice

1 clove garlic, minced

¼ teaspoon coarse kosher salt

¼ cup (60 ml) extra-virgin olive oil

2 tablespoons to ¼ cup (30 to 60 ml) water, as needed

FOR THE BITES:

Nonstick cooking spray or oil spray

1 cup (200 g) packed cooked spelt berries (or similar grain, like kamut)

1 cup (185 g) cooked cannellini beans

¼ cup (60 g) pesto, plus extra for serving

¼ to ½ cup (20 to 40 g) whole-wheat panko bread crumbs, as needed

A few grinds black peppercorn

½ teaspoon coarse kosher salt

To make the pesto: Place the basil, spinach, broth powder, lemon juice, garlic, and salt in a food processor or blender. Pulse a few times to chop. Slowly drizzle in the oil and add water, as needed, until the mixture is well combined, smooth, and neither too thick nor too thin. Store in an airtight jar in the refrigerator until ready to use for up to 3 days.

To make the bites: Preheat the oven to 350°F (180°C, or gas mark 4). Lightly coat a mini muffin tin with cooking spray.

In a large bowl, mash together the cooked spelt, beans, pesto, pepper, and salt. Stir ¼ cup (20 g) of bread crumbs into the mixture: It should be easy to form into not-too-dry, not-too-wet ball shapes with the hands. Add the remaining ¼ cup (20 g), if needed, as the moisture level depends on how tender the beans are. Spoon out 1 packed tablespoon (22 g) of mixture, shape into a ball and place in the prepared tin. Repeat with remaining bites, and lightly coat tops with cooking spray. You should get 24 bites in all, but this number can vary slightly. Bake 15 minutes and flip carefully. Bake for another 10 to 15 minutes until firm. Let stand at least 5 minutes before serving with extra pesto.

YIELD: 22 to 24 bites, ¾ cup plus 2 tablespoons (210 g) pesto

Dirty Rice Bites with Mango Salsa

▶ **GRAIN**: BROWN RICE ▶ SOY-FREE POTENTIAL ▶ QUICK AND EASY

Bring on the Bayou! These fritter bites are easy to make and quick to disappear. We've paired them with a zesty mango-and-tomato salsa—perfect for dunking!

FOR THE MANGO SALSA:

½ cup (80 g) minced fresh mango

½ cup (90 g) chopped tomato

1 tablespoon plus 1 teaspoon (13 g) minced shallot

1 teaspoon minced fresh parsley

¼ seeded, minced jalapeño, or to taste

1 teaspoon balsamic vinegar

Hot sauce

Salt and pepper

FOR THE DIRTY RICE BITES:

1 cup (107 g) Dirty Rice (page 107)

1 cup (182 g) prepared white beans (such as Navy or Great Northern), mashed

½ cup (60 g) all-purpose flour

High heat neutral-flavored oil, for cooking

To make the salsa: Combine the mango, tomato, shallot, parsley, jalapeño, and vinegar in a small bowl. Season to taste with the hot sauce, salt, and pepper. Set aside to let the flavors blend. The salsa may be made ahead of time and refrigerated airtight for up to 2 days. If refrigerated, bring the salsa to room temperature before serving.

To make the bites: Combine the rice and mashed beans in a medium-size bowl. Stir together well. Scoop 2 tablespoons (40 g) of the mixture and form into a small round patty, about 2 inches (5 cm) across. Place on a baking sheet. When all the bites are formed, heat a thin layer of oil in a large skillet over medium heat. Working in batches, dredge the bites in the flour, then put in the hot oil. Cook for 4 to 5 minutes until nicely browned. Turn over to cook the second side for 3 to 5 minutes until browned. Continue until all of the bites are cooked. Serve with the salsa.

YIELD: 14 bites, generous 1 cup (160 g) salsa

Dirty Rice

▶ **GRAIN:** BROWN RICE/WILD RICE BLEND ▶ GLUTEN-FREE POTENTIAL
▶ SOY-FREE POTENTIAL

For flavorful-but-easy meals look no further than the "new" grains that are popping up on store shelves. Here, we've enhanced one of our recent finds: a brown and wild rice blend. With the holy trinity of New Orleans cuisine, this one is exceptional beside baked tofu, grilled seitan, or—of course—beans!

1 tablespoon (15 ml) olive oil

½ cup (80 g) minced onion

¼ cup (30 g) minced celery

¼ cup (30 g) minced green bell pepper

2 cloves garlic, minced

1 teaspoon Cajun spice blend

1 teaspoon dry poultry seasoning

¼ teaspoon cayenne pepper, optional

¼ teaspoon dried thyme

½ teaspoon salt (see Recipe Note)

1 cup (180 g) wild rice/brown rice blend

2 cups (470 ml) water

Heat the oil in a lidded medium-size saucepan over medium heat. Add the onion, celery, pepper, garlic, spices, salt, and rice. Stir to coat and cook for 3 to 5 minutes, until fragrant. Add the water and bring to a boil. Cover and reduce to simmer. Cook for 35 to 45 minutes until the rice is tender.

YIELD: 4 side servings

Recipe Note

If the Cajun spice blend is salty, reduce or eliminate the salt.

Harissa Veggies and Rice Skillet

▶ **GRAIN**: BROWN RICE ▶ GLUTEN-FREE POTENTIAL ▶ QUICK AND EASY
▶ SOY-FREE POTENTIAL

As it is written, this recipe is quite mild, despite the harissa. You can adjust its quantity to taste for spicier results. This delicious, ready-in-a-snap rice would be perfect served alongside your favorite bean recipe. The benefit of adding beans is that your meal would now be turned into a filling, complete protein, in one fell swoop.

1 tablespoon (15 ml) toasted sesame oil

5 tablespoons (50 g) minced shallot

1 tablespoon (10 g) minced garlic

1 bell pepper (any color), seeded and chopped

Fine sea salt, to taste

1 teaspoon ground cumin

2 teaspoons (4 g) dry harissa blend or paste, to taste

1 tablespoon (15 ml) fresh lemon juice

1 cup (164 g) frozen corn kernels, rinsed to thaw slightly

¾ cup (188 g) chopped tomato with juice (such as Pomi)

1 tablespoon (8 g) nutritional yeast

2 slightly heaping cups (420 g) cooked and chilled brown rice of choice

Fresh cilantro or parsley leaves, for garnish

Lemon wedges, for garnish

Place the oil, shallot, garlic, and bell pepper in a large skillet. Heat on medium-high and cook, stirring occasionally, until the vegetables just start to soften, about 4 minutes. Add salt to taste, cumin, and harissa. Sauté for another minute. Add the lemon juice and corn, folding to combine. Sauté for another minute. Add the tomatoes, nutritional yeast, and rice. Cook uncovered on medium-low heat for 8 minutes until heated through and to let the flavors meld. Adjust seasoning, if needed. Garnish with fresh herb of choice and lemon wedges.

YIELD: 4 side servings

Greek Barley

▶ GRAIN: BARLEY ▶ SOY-FREE POTENTIAL

We vegans love our potlucks! Several testers thought this would be a terrific make-and-take dish. We agree. It's a customizable recipe, so be sure to add more of your favorites—whether it's the olives or the artichoke hearts. If we're lucky enough to have a handful of homegrown cherry tomatoes, we add those, too.

1 cup (157 g) prepared barley, cooled

2 tablespoons (20 g) minced red onion

4 pitted kalamata olives, chopped

2 green olives, chopped

2 tablespoons (23 g) jarred roasted red bell pepper, chopped

1 water-packed artichoke heart, chopped

2 teaspoons (3 g) minced fresh parsley

2 teaspoons (10 ml) fresh lemon juice

¼ teaspoon dried oregano, crumbled

¼ teaspoon evaporated cane juice

Salt and pepper

Put the barley, onion, olives, red pepper, artichoke heart, and parsley in a medium-size bowl.

Whisk the lemon juice, oregano, and evaporated cane juice together in a small bowl. Pour over the barley. Let sit 30 minutes for the flavors to meld or cover and refrigerate. Taste and adjust the seasonings before serving.

YIELD: 1¾ cups (270 g)

Jasmine Rice Kedgeree

▶ **GRAIN:** BROWN RICE ▶ GLUTEN-FREE POTENTIAL ▶ SOY-FREE POTENTIAL

Kedgeree is an Anglo-Indian dish that often contains fish. Our version is happily seafood-free here. We're quite fond of jasmine rice and of its faint floral flavor, but if you prefer brown basmati rice, it will work quite well, too. (Adjust cooking liquid amount and cooking time, if needed.) Because no dish is complete without tons of vegetables, be sure to serve the kedgeree with a generous amount of roasted cauliflower or broccoli!

1 tablespoon (15 ml) grapeseed or olive oil, divided

1 cup (180 g) dry brown jasmine rice, rinsed and drained

1¾ cups (415 ml) water

1 yellow onion, peeled and chopped

Generous ¼ teaspoon smoked or regular fine sea salt, to taste

½ teaspoon ground cumin

½ teaspoon ground coriander

¼ teaspoon ground turmeric

¼ teaspoon garam masala

⅛ teaspoon cayenne pepper, to taste, optional

1 tablespoon (17 g) tomato paste

2 cloves garlic, minced

Splash vegan dry white wine or mirin

1½ cups (201 g) thawed green peas

Combine 1½ teaspoons oil, rice, and water in a large skillet. Bring to a boil, cover, and simmer until the liquid is absorbed, 30 to 35 minutes. Let stand covered away from the heat for 10 minutes, then fluff with a fork.

While the rice cooks, heat the remaining 1½ teaspoons of oil in another large skillet. Add the onion and sauté on medium-high heat until browned, about 8 to 10 minutes, stirring occasionally. Adjust the heat, if needed, to make sure the onion doesn't burn. Add the salt, cumin, coriander, turmeric, garam masala, cayenne pepper if using, tomato paste, and garlic. Stir quickly just to combine. The skillet will be hot, so add a splash of wine or mirin immediately after stirring to make sure this mixture stays moist and doesn't burn, then cook 1 minute. Stir the peas into the onion-and-spice mixture. Cook for 1 or 2 minutes just until the peas are heated through. Stir the onion-and-spice mixture into the rice. Serve with roasted vegetables on the side. Leftovers reheat well, so this is a dish that can be prepared ahead of time, if needed. Store cooled leftovers in an airtight container in the refrigerator for up to 4 days.

YIELD: 4 to 6 side servings

Green Beans and Bulgur

▶ **GRAIN**: BULGUR ▶ SOY-FREE POTENTIAL ▶ QUICK AND EASY

Tender-yet-crunchy green beans make every bite of this bulgur dish delectable. It's a simple, almost rustic dish, and it is a wonderful side for baked tofu or grilled portobello mushrooms.

1 cup (160 g) dry bulgur

2 cups (470 ml) water

1 tablespoon (15 ml) olive oil

2 cups (240 g) 1-inch (2.5 cm) pieces green beans

¼ cup (40 g) chopped shallot

4 cloves garlic, minced

½ cup (48 g) grated carrots

2 teaspoons (5 g) paprika

1 teaspoon dried Italian seasoning

1 teaspoon dried thyme

¼ teaspoon dried rosemary

Salt and pepper

Combine the bulgur and water in a medium-size saucepan. Bring to a boil, then reduce the heat to simmer and cover. Cook for 12 to 15 minutes or until tender. If any liquid remains, drain the bulgur. Set aside.

Heat the oil in a large skillet over medium-high heat. Add the green beans and shallot and cook for 2 to 3 minutes until the beans are bright green, but do not overcook. Add the garlic, carrots, paprika, Italian seasoning, and thyme. Cook for 2 minutes longer. Add the bulgur and stir. Cook for 3 to 4 minutes or until heated through and combined. Season to taste with salt and pepper.

YIELD: 6 side servings

Savory Stuffed Apples

▶ **GRAIN**: EINKORN

This tasty side dish really struts its stuff beside a seitan cutlet. The baking time will vary depending on both the size and the variety of the apples. Try to choose apples that are similar in size for consistency in baking. As far as the grain goes, barley, farro, or freekeh would be good stand-ins for the einkorn.

1 cup (208 g) dry einkorn

1 tablespoon plus 1 teaspoon (13 g) minced shallot

2 teaspoons (12 g) dark miso (South River Garlic Red Pepper is a favorite)

2 teaspoons (10 ml) seasoned rice vinegar

1 teaspoon tahini paste

¼ teaspoon minced fresh rosemary, or ½ teaspoon dried

Salt and pepper

4 McIntosh, Melrose, or other sturdy baking apples, cored

Prepare the grain according to the chart, page 15. Preheat the oven to 400°F (200°C, or gas mark 6).

Mix together the einkorn, shallot, miso, vinegar, and tahini paste in a medium-size bowl. Season to taste with salt and pepper. Pack the grain mixture evenly into the cored apples, patting any extra on top. Bake for 15 minutes. If the apples are not tender, cover loosely with foil and bake for 15 minutes longer or until the apples are tender. The size of the apples will determine the baking time.

YIELD: 4 servings

Corn-oa

▶ **GRAIN**: QUINOA ▶ GLUTEN-FREE POTENTIAL ▶ SOY-FREE POTENTIAL

Sure, rice is great for a Mexican-themed dinner, but it's time to shake it up. While our grain of choice here is *very* authentic, we'll admit that the way we use it isn't. The chipotle is highly recommended, but not absolutely necessary. Leftovers are highly recommended, too, because you will definitely want to make the Super-Quick Quinoa and Black Bean Sliders (page 86).

2 cups (470 ml) water

½ to 1 chipotle pepper in adobo

1 tablespoon (15 ml) olive oil

½ cup (80 g) minced onion

¼ cup (38 g) minced green bell peppers

5 cherry tomatoes, cut into quarters

3 to 4 cloves garlic, minced

1 cup (164 g) frozen corn kernels, run under hot water to thaw

1 cup (173 g) dry quinoa

1 teaspoon fine sea salt

¼ teaspoon ground black pepper

Blend the chipotle with the water in a blender. Set aside.

Heat the oil in a medium-size saucepan over medium heat. Add the onion, pepper, and tomatoes. Cook and stir until softened, 3 to 4 minutes. Stir in the garlic and corn, and cook 2 minutes longer. Stir in the quinoa, salt, pepper, and water. Bring to a boil, cover, and reduce the heat. Simmer for 20 to 25 minutes, or until the tails have popped and the water is absorbed.

YIELD: 4 side servings

Spinach and Basil Quinoa

▶ **GRAIN**: QUINOA ▶ GLUTEN-FREE POTENTIAL ▶ QUICK AND EASY

The fresh spinach and basil shine in this simple, easy side dish. If you have leftovers, refrigerate them airtight. Check the seasonings when serving the leftovers . . . as a salad!

2 tablespoons (30 ml) white wine vinegar

1 tablespoon (15 ml) tamari

2 cloves garlic, minced

2 teaspoons (6 g) nutritional yeast

½ teaspoon dried thyme

Pinch red pepper flakes, optional

½ cup (92 g) dry quinoa

Handful baby spinach, chopped

3 tablespoons (8 g) chopped fresh basil

2 tablespoons (12 g) minced scallion

Salt and pepper

Whisk the vinegar, tamari, garlic, nutritional yeast, thyme, and red pepper flakes together in a small bowl. Set aside.

Cook the quinoa according to the package directions. Drain and return to the saucepan. Stir in the spinach, basil, scallion, and the vinegar mixture. Season to taste with salt and pepper.

YIELD: 4 side servings

Recipe Note

Looking for a slightly more substantial dish that still screams "fresh!"? Try adding 1½ cups (266 g) cooked white beans of choice, such as cannellini or navy beans. Quartered cherry tomatoes are an awesome addition, too.

Cabbage Pilaf

▶ **GRAIN**: FREEKEH ▶ SOY-FREE POTENTIAL
▶ QUICK AND EASY

Crisp vegetables spike the grain of your choice in this quick-to-prepare, fresh-tasting side dish. We opt for freekeh here, but feel free to substitute barley, einkorn, or kamut, if you prefer.

Heat the oil in a large skillet over medium heat. Add the onion, bell pepper, and cabbage. Cook, stirring occasionally, for 4 minutes until soft. Add the carrots, herbes de Provence, and freekeh. Cook, stirring, until heated throughout. Stir in the lemon juice and parsley. Season to taste with salt and pepper.

YIELD: 4 side servings

1 tablespoon (15 ml) olive oil

½ cup (80 g) chopped onion

⅓ cup (49 g) chopped red bell pepper

2 cups (154 g) chopped cabbage

½ cup (56 g) grated carrots

½ teaspoon dried herbes de Provence (see Recipe Note)

2 cups (336 g) cooked freekeh

Juice from ½ lemon

1 tablespoon (3 g) minced fresh parsley

Salt and pepper

Recipe Note

A few of our testers felt that the lavender component in the herbes de Provence blend was overwhelming. Tami uses Penzey's brand and is happy with it, but if you are lavender-hesitant, substitute dried Italian seasoning.

Tahini-Topped Kamut and Brussels Sprouts

▶ GRAIN: KAMUT ▶ SOY-FREE POTENTIAL

Brussels sprouts are one of our favorites. We just can't get enough of them. We're betting you feel the same . . . so we're sharing our tangy, tahini-topped version of wilted brussels sprouts enhanced by kamut and za'atar.

FOR THE BOWL BASE:

1 teaspoon olive oil

12 ounces (340 g) brussels sprouts, thinly sliced

Salt and pepper

1 cup (184 g) kamut, cooked, and cooled

¾ cup (120 g) minced carrot

½ cup (76 g) minced onion

Juice of 1 lemon

1 to 2 tablespoons (2 to 4 g) za'atar seasoning

FOR THE DRESSING:

½ cup (120 ml) vegetable broth

2 tablespoons to ¼ cup (30 ml to 60 ml) white wine vinegar

1 tablespoon plus 1 teaspoon (20 g) tahini paste

2 teaspoons (8 g) Dijon mustard

2 teaspoons (10 g) toasted sesame oil

½ to 1 teaspoon pure maple syrup

2 cloves garlic

To make the bowl base: Heat the oil in a large skillet over medium-high heat. Add the brussels sprouts and season with salt and pepper. Cook, stirring occasionally, until wilted and some are blackened, 6 to 8 minutes. Transfer to a bowl. When cool, stir in the remaining bowl base ingredients, adding the za'atar to taste.

To make the dressing: Combine all the ingredients in a small high-powered blender. Process until smooth. Pour over the bowl to taste, reserving some of the dressing if not serving immediately. The bowl can be covered and refrigerated for up to 3 days. Add extra dressing to moisten when serving.

YIELD: 4 side servings

Recipe Note

To make this a meal, stir in 1 can (15 ounces, or 425 g) of chickpeas, rinsed and drained. Adjust the seasonings as needed.

Sesame Purple Rice

▶ **GRAIN:** BLACK RICE ▶ GLUTEN-FREE POTENTIAL

Black rice cooks into a beautiful, dark-purple hue. We've matched it with purple carrots, but any carrot will do. If you cannot find black rice, use wild rice or any brown rice (or a combination of both) instead. Simply change the cooking time and method accordingly. Maca powder is a nutrition-filled dried root, but nutritional yeast can be used in its place if it's unavailable or cost prohibitive.

1 cup (180 g) dry black rice, rinsed and drained

2 tablespoons (32 g) tahini paste

2 tablespoons (30 ml) water

1 tablespoon (15 ml) seasoned rice vinegar

1 tablespoon (15 ml) fresh lemon juice

1½ teaspoons tamari

1½ teaspoons white miso

1 teaspoon maca powder or nutritional yeast (optional)

Pinch cayenne pepper, to taste, optional

1 teaspoon agave nectar or brown rice syrup

1½ teaspoons toasted sesame oil

9 ounces (about 4, or 255 g) carrots, peeled and thinly sliced into half-moons

¼ cup (20 g) chopped scallion

1 to 2 cloves garlic, minced

1 cup (134 g) frozen green peas or (155 g) shelled edamame, thawed

Toasted sesame seeds or cashews, for garnish

Place the rice in a medium pot. Cover with an extra 2 inches (5 cm) water. Bring to a boil and cook uncovered on medium heat until al dente, about 25 minutes. Stir occasionally. Drain in a sieve and quickly rinse with cold water. Place the sieve on top of the pot to further drain and cool.

While the rice is cooking, place the tahini, water, vinegar, lemon juice, tamari, miso, maca powder, cayenne pepper if using, and agave in a small bowl. Whisk to thoroughly combine. Set aside.

Place the oil, carrots, and scallion in a large skillet. Cook on medium heat until tender, about 6 to 8 minutes. Add the garlic and cook another minute. Whisk the tahini sauce again. Pour the desired quantity on top of carrots, folding to combine. Fold the cooled rice into the preparation and cook until heated through, about 4 minutes. Add the peas and cook another minute. (Alternatively, you can combine carrots, rice, and peas, and slowly heat the sauce on the side, serving with warm sauce drizzled over each portion for an even prettier outcome.) Garnish with sesame seeds. We love to serve this with cooked-to-crisp green or red cabbage on the side. If you have sauce leftovers, store in an airtight container in the refrigerator for up to 4 days.

YIELD: 4 side servings, ½ cup (120 ml) sauce

Easy Cheesy Baked Grits

▶ **GRAIN**: POLENTA

This hearty dish is a big hit for brunch, but it's savory enough to be a sensational side for dinner. Grits are sometimes thought to be a bit touchy to cook, but our baked version couldn't be easier.

Nonstick cooking spray

2 cups (470 ml) plain, unsweetened vegan milk

1½ cups (355 ml) vegetable broth

¾ cup (107 g) sauerkraut, drained but not squeezed

½ cup (70 g) raw cashews

⅓ cup (50 g) minced onion

⅓ cup (40 g) nutritional yeast

1 tablespoon (15 ml) apple cider vinegar

1 tablespoon (18 g) light miso

1 tablespoon (15 ml) olive oil

2 cloves garlic

1 teaspoon Dijon mustard

1 teaspoon fine sea salt

½ teaspoon ground white pepper

1 cup (140 g) polenta (grits)

Ground black pepper, to taste

Preheat the oven to 350°F (180°C, or gas mark 4). Lightly spray a 9 x 13-inch (23 x 33 cm) baking dish with cooking spray.

Combine the milk, broth, sauerkraut, cashews, onion, nutritional yeast, vinegar, miso, olive oil, garlic, mustard, salt, and white pepper in a high-powered blender. Process until very smooth. Pour into a medium-size saucepan. Bring to a boil over medium heat. Gently pour the grits into the liquid, whisking continuously. Reduce to a simmer and cook, whisking, for 5 minutes. Taste and adjust the seasonings, adding the black pepper. Pour into the pre-pared baking dish. Bake for 25 minutes until set. Let cool 5 minutes before serving.

YIELD: 1 (9-inch, or 23 cm) dish

Recipe Notes

- For firmer grits, reduce the water by ¼ cup (60 ml).

- Customize your grits! Add finely minced hot or bell peppers, slivered greens, or grated carrot after whisking in the grits.

Spiced Einkorn

▶ GRAIN: EINKORN ▶ SOY-FREE POTENTIAL

We all need more extra-easy, yet always pleasing, side dishes in our repertoires. This one is sensational beside baked tofu or some saucy seitan. As all harissa pastes vary, we choose a spicy one here. Cook to your own tastes.

1 tablespoon (15 ml) olive oil

¼ cup (40 g) minced shallot

1 carrot, peeled and grated

2 teaspoons (10 g) harissa paste, more to taste

1 teaspoon berbere, more to taste

½ teaspoon fine sea salt

1 cup (208 g) dry einkorn, or grain of choice

2 teaspoons (10 ml) fresh lemon juice, or to taste

2 cups (470 ml) water

Heat the oil, shallot, carrot, harissa, berbere, and salt in a small, heavy-bottomed pot that also has a lid, over medium heat. Add the grain and stir to coat the grains, cook for 3 to 4 minutes until fragrant. Add the lemon juice and water and bring to a boil, cover, and reduce the heat to simmer. Cook, stirring occasionally, for 35 to 40 minutes or until the grain is tender. Taste and adjust the seasoning.

YIELD: 4 side servings

Recipe Notes

- Any grain you like can be substituted in this recipe, but be sure to adjust the amount of water and the cooking time accordingly.

- Both berbere and harissa are available in the ethnic aisles of most grocery stores. Also, both are spicy, so cook to taste!

Burst Tomato Farro

▸ **GRAIN**: FARRO ▸ SOY-FREE POTENTIAL ▸ QUICK AND EASY

Looking for a quick, soul-satisfying lunch? You've just found it. Quick, easy, and full of flavor, this one might end up in regular rotation at your house.

1 cup (172 g) dry farro

2½ cups (590 ml) water

1 tablespoon (15 ml) olive oil

2 packages (10 ounces, or 280 g each) grape or cherry tomatoes

5 cloves garlic, sliced

½ teaspoon dried thyme

Salt and pepper

Handful fresh basil leaves, thinly cut, for garnish

1 tablespoon plus 1 teaspoon (20 ml) balsamic reduction (see Recipe Note)

Combine the farro and water in a medium-size saucepan. Bring to a boil, then reduce to simmer. Cook until tender, 20 to 30 minutes. Set aside.

Heat the oil in a large skillet over medium-high heat. Add the tomatoes and toss to coat. Cook for 5 to 6 minutes, stirring occasionally, until the tomatoes just start to get some black spots and split a little. The goal is to keep the tomatoes relatively whole, rather than as a sauce. Add the garlic and thyme and cook for 1 minute, or until the garlic is very lightly browned. Stir constantly so the garlic doesn't burn. Remove from the heat. Season with salt and pepper to taste.

To serve, divide the farro between 4 plates and place the tomatoes and garlic around the farro. Garnish with the basil, and drizzle each plate with about 1 teaspoon of the balsamic reduction.

YIELD: 4 servings

Recipe Note

To make a balsamic reduction, pour ½ cup (120 ml) of balsamic vinegar in a small saucepan. Bring to a boil, then reduce the heat to simmer. Cook for 10 minutes, stirring occasionally. As the vinegar thickens and reduces, it is more likely to be burn. For a thicker syrup, cook for 15 minutes. Store the extra airtight in the refrigerator for up 2 months. Drizzle it over roasted vegetables or use it in a salad dressing. Yields ¼ cup (60 ml)

Asian-Style Freekeh

▶ **GRAIN**: FREEKEH (WHOLE) ▶ QUICK AND EASY

Versatile dish, ahoy! We love freekeh, but you can use barley, rice, or more sturdy freekeh-like grains such as kamut, wheat berries, or spelt. Then, pair your grain with the greens you love the most (cooking extra on the side because there can never be too much). Make it even heartier by pairing it with your favorite vegan protein (see Recipe Notes).

2 cups (300 g) cooked whole freekeh (cooked in broth)

1 cup (approximately 40 g) packed minced fresh kale, spinach, or other similar leafy green

1 tablespoon (15 ml) seasoned rice wine vinegar

1½ teaspoons toasted sesame oil

1½ teaspoons brown rice syrup or agave nectar, optional

2 teaspoons (12 g) white miso

2 teaspoons (10 ml) tamari

1 large clove garlic, grated or pressed

Couple grates fresh ginger, to taste

2½ tablespoons (15 g) minced scallion

¼ cup (37 g) dry roasted peanuts or cashews, coarsely chopped

Place the freekeh and minced greens in a large skillet. In a small bowl, whisk to combine the vinegar, oil, sweetener, miso, tamari, garlic, and ginger. Gently fold the dressing and scallion into the skillet. Sauté to heat through, allow the flavors to meld, and wilt the greens, about 5 minutes. Adjust seasoning, if needed. Sprinkle with chopped nuts upon serving.

YIELD: 2 to 3 side servings

Recipe Notes

• We love to serve this with 1 pound (454 g) of super-firm tofu cut into small cubes, baked or panfried on medium-high heat in a minimal amount of peanut oil until crispy (about 10 minutes, with frequent stirring). Add ½ teaspoon of coarse kosher salt and ½ teaspoon liquid smoke during the last 5 minutes of cooking time. Baked tempeh would be great, too.

• Fresh cubes of perfectly ripe pineapple also make for a great accompaniment if you enjoy the sweet and savory combination.

• Be sure to serve with more wilted greens on the side!

5

GREAT GRAIN SOUPS AND SALADS

**Grains can find their way into any course.
Don't believe us? Turn the page and see.**

Soups and salads get a lot of mileage in our homes. What else can you serve as a starter, side, or a meal in itself? With lots of flavor, vegetables, and grain choices, these recipes will fit the menu—and your lifestyle—with flying colors.

Rustic Vegetable Stew

▶ GRAIN: BARLEY

When the winds of winter are howling, we turn to this comfort-food favorite. We've had it over several grains, and it's hard to go wrong. So pick your favorite and get cooking. With French leanings, tender vegetables, and hearty seitan (or beans), this stew sticks to your ribs.

1 tablespoon (15 ml) olive oil

2 turnips, peeled, cut into 1-inch (2.5 cm) pieces

2 medium carrots, peeled, cut into 1-inch (2.5 cm) pieces

1 large leek, white part only, cut in half lengthwise, then into 1-inch (2.5 cm) half rounds

1 parsnip, peeled, cut into 1-inch (2.5 cm) chunks

8 ounces (227 g) Kind-to-Cows Seitan (page 168), cut into 1-inch (2.5 cm) pieces

1 medium tomato, chopped

4 cloves garlic, minced

1 teaspoon ground dried porcini mushrooms (see Recipe Note)

½ teaspoon herbes de Provence

½ teaspoon dried thyme

Pinch dried rosemary

¼ cup (60 ml) dry red wine or additional broth

3 cups (705 ml) vegetable broth

1 tablespoon (15 ml) tamari

1 beef-style vegan bouillon cube

1-inch (2.5 cm) slice of cabbage, cut into 1-inch (2.5 cm) pieces

Salt and pepper

1 cup (157 g) prepared barley, einkorn, farro, freekeh, or kamut

Heat the oil in a large soup pot over medium heat. Add the turnips, carrots, leek, and parsnip. Cook, stirring occasionally, for 3 to 5 minutes. Add the seitan, tomato, garlic, porcini powder, herbes de Provence, and rosemary. Cook for 3 to 4 minutes, stirring occasionally, until fragrant. Add the wine, broth, tamari, and bouillon. Reduce the heat to simmer and cook for 20 minutes, stirring occasionally.

Check one of the vegetables, it should be almost tender. Add the cabbage and cook for 10 minutes longer, or until the vegetables are tender but still have bite. Season to taste with salt and pepper.

To serve, scoop ¼ cup (39 g) of the grain in each bowl. Ladle the soup over the grain.

YIELD: 4 servings

Recipe Notes

- To make porcini powder, grind dried porcini mushrooms in a coffee or spice grinder until powdered. The powder can be used in any dish where an earthy flavor is needed. Store the powder airtight for up to 3 months.

- If you prefer, omit the seitan and add 1½ cups (266 g) cooked white beans with the cabbage, instead.

Moroccan Wheatball Stew with Couscous

▶ **GRAIN**: BULGUR ▶ QUICK AND EASY

We've gone wild for these wheatballs and all their variations! Keep a batch or two in the freezer, and you can have dinner on the table in no time! Here, we've matched them with traditional Moroccan flavors and, of course, couscous.

1 tablespoon (15 ml) olive oil

½ onion, chopped into 1-inch (2.5 cm) pieces

¼ head cauliflower cut into bite-size florets

½ any color bell pepper, cut into 1-inch (2.5 cm) pieces

2 medium carrots, peeled, cut into 1-inch (2.5 cm) pieces

1 small zucchini, cut into 1-inch (2.5 cm) pieces

½ jalapeño pepper, minced, optional

3 cloves garlic, minced

1 teaspoon minced fresh ginger

1 teaspoon ground cinnamon

1 teaspoon ground cumin

½ teaspoon ground allspice

¼ teaspoon cayenne pepper, more to taste

½ teaspoon ground turmeric

½ recipe Moroccan Wheatballs (page 91)

2 plum tomatoes, chopped

1 cup (235 ml) vegetable broth

2 tablespoons (30 ml) fresh orange juice

2 tablespoons (18 g) dark raisins

1 beef-flavored bouillon cube

Salt and pepper

Prepared couscous, for serving

Heat the oil in a large skillet over medium heat. Add the onion through the turmeric. Cook, stirring, for 3 to 4 minutes until fragrant. Add the wheatballs and cook for 3 to 4 minutes longer. Add the tomatoes, broth, orange juice, raisins, and bouillon cube. Cover and reduce to simmer.

Cook for 20 minutes until the wheatballs are cooked through. Season to taste with salt and pepper. Serve over couscous.

YIELD: 4 servings

Pick-Your-Grain Miso Soup

▶ **GRAIN**: CHOICE ▶ GLUTEN-FREE POTENTIAL

This one is a throwback to Tami's macrobiotic days way back in the 1980s. We loved having miso soup for breakfast and have just started doing it again. Please make your own broth—the success of this soup depends on it.

Bag of frozen vegetable scraps
(see Recipe Note)

8 cups (2 L) water

¼ cup (60 ml) white wine, or
additional broth

2 tablespoons (30 ml) tamari

6 cloves garlic, mashed

1-inch (2.5 cm) piece of ginger,
roughly chopped

Few dried porcini mushrooms, optional

Handful fresh parsley (on stems),
or 1 tablespoon (4 g) dried

Half handful fresh thyme (on stems),
or 2 teaspoons (3 g) dried

½ stem fresh rosemary, or ¼ teaspoon
dried

2 dried bay leaves

1 teaspoon white peppercorns

Pinch red pepper flakes, optional

Salt and pepper

FOR EACH SERVING OF MISO SOUP:

1 cup (235 ml) homemade broth

3 tablespoons (27 grams, weight will
vary) prepared grain of choice

1 teaspoon savory miso, such as South
River Red Pepper and Garlic Miso

Minced scallions, for garnish

Combine all of the ingredients in a large soup pot. Bring the mixture to a boil, then cover and reduce to a gentle simmer. Cook for 1½ hours. Let cool slightly, then pour into a large bowl using a strainer to catch the vegetables and herbs. Divide into containers for storage and refrigerate airtight for 1 week or freeze up to 3 months.

For each serving of miso soup: Heat the broth and grain in a small saucepan over high heat. Bring to a boil, then turn off. Stir in the miso until dissolved. Top the serving with the scallions.

YIELD: 6 to 8 servings

Recipe Note

Tami puts most of her vegetables scraps in a gallon-size resealable bag in the freezer, adding to the bag daily as a part of meal preparation. Vegetables from the onion family are ideal, as are carrots and celery. Adding some greens is great, but don't overdo it on vegetables from the cabbage family, which will over-power the flavor of the broth.

Hummus-in-the-Making Kamut Stew

▶ GRAIN: KAMUT

A little stumped whether it wants to call itself soup or stew, this hearty "st-oup" turned out to be a surprise favorite among testers. Serve it with pita bread if you'd like. If kamut isn't available, use wheat berries or any grain with a similarly sturdy texture. The tiny drizzle of toasted sesame oil upon serving is what takes this stoup from really good to outstanding—so don't skip it!

11 ounces (312 g) carrots, trimmed, peeled, and diced (about 4 carrots)

½ cup (80 g) chopped shallot

1 tablespoon (10 g) minced garlic

2 tablespoons (16 g) Broth Powder (page 167), divided

¼ cup (60 ml) fresh lemon juice, divided

1 teaspoon dry harissa blend or paste, to taste

1 cup (164 g) cooked chickpeas

1¼ cups (215 g) cooked kamut (al dente)

3⅓ cups (785 ml) water

¼ cup (64 g) tahini paste

2 tablespoons (36 g) white miso

Salt

Toasted sesame oil, to drizzle

In a large pot, place the carrots, shallot, garlic, 1 tablespoon (8 g) broth powder, and 2 tablespoons (30 ml) lemon juice. Cook on medium heat for 2 minutes. Cover with a lid, and cook until the carrots just start to soften. This will depend on the carrots used, about 6 and 10 minutes. Stir occasionally and add a splash of water, if needed, to keep the veggies from sticking to the pot. Add harissa, chickpeas, kamut. Cook another 2 minutes. Add the water and bring to a gentle boil. Lower the heat to medium again and simmer uncovered for 10 minutes, stirring occasionally. Remove ¼ cup (60 ml) of cooking broth.

In a medium bowl, whisk to combine the tahini, miso, remaining 2 tablespoons (30 ml) lemon juice, remaining tablespoon (8 g) broth powder, and the cooking broth removed from the pot. (Tahini paste sometimes curdles when added to hot liquid. This step and the upcoming simmering time will help prevent that.) Pour the mixture into the soup. Simmer uncovered for 15 to 20 minutes until slightly thickened and fragrant and the carrots are fully tender. Adjust seasoning, if needed. Let stand 15 minutes before serving, ideally. Drizzle each serving with a tiny bit of sesame oil.

YIELD: 4 servings

Sort-of-Like-a-Samosa Soup

▶ GRAIN: BULGUR

Our Indian-inspired meatball soup is a bowlful of perfectly seasoned tomatoey broth, tender vegetables, and tasty wheatballs. So grab those wheatballs from the freezer and get ready for a bold-flavored, soul-warming soup in just over 30 minutes.

1 tablespoon (15 ml) olive oil

1 large onion, chopped

5 cloves garlic, minced

2 teaspoons (5 g) grated fresh ginger

2 teaspoons (4 g) ground coriander

2 teaspoons (5 g) ground cumin

2 teaspoons (4 g) curry powder (hot or mild)

½ teaspoon ground cinnamon

8 small golden potatoes, diced

2 large carrots, peeled and chopped

½ cup (65 g) fresh green peas, optional

1 jalapeño pepper, seeded, and minced

1 recipe Indian Wheatballs (page 91)

5 cups (1.2 L) vegetable broth

1 can (15 ounces, or 425 g) tomato sauce

Salt and pepper

Green chutney, for garnish

Heat the oil in a large soup pot over medium heat. Add the onion, garlic, ginger, coriander, cumin, curry powder, cinnamon, and a pinch of salt. Cook, stirring occasionally, for 3 to 4 minutes until fragrant. Add the potatoes, carrots, peas, jalapeño, wheatballs, broth, and tomato sauce. Bring to a boil, then reduce to simmer. Cook, stirring occasionally, for 30 minutes. The wheatballs should be cooked through and the vegetables tender. Season to taste with salt and pepper. Garnish servings with chutney.

YIELD: 6 servings

Recipe Note

For a thicker soup base, omit the tomato sauce and add 1 can (6 ounces, or 170 g) tomato paste.

Turkish Bride Soup

▶ GRAIN: BULGUR ▶ SOY-FREE POTENTIAL

This thick and homey dish is more stew than soup, but because it is a traditional recipe, we're honoring its history. The story behind the soup is that a Turkish widow, Ezo, prepared it to please her *second* mother-in-law—without success. Now, the soup is served at Turkish weddings. One note on the mint: We will admit to not being fans of mint, so we've made it optional.

1 tablespoon (15 ml) olive oil

1 cup (160 g) finely minced onion

1 teaspoon fine sea salt

1 teaspoon ground cumin

1 teaspoon dried oregano

1 teaspoon paprika

½ teaspoon dried mint, or to taste (See headnote)

¼ teaspoon red pepper flakes, or to taste

¾ cup (141 g) dry bulgur

½ cup (96 g) split red lentils, picked over and rinsed

5 cups (1.2 L) vegetable broth

1 can (15 ounces, or 425 g) fire-roasted, crushed tomatoes

Juice from ½ lemon

1 bunch (8 ounces, or 227 g) Swiss chard, stems removed, leaves thinly sliced

Salt and pepper

1 tablespoon (9 g) toasted pine nuts

Heat the oil in soup pot over medium heat. Add the onion and salt. Cook for 4 to 6 minutes, stirring occasionally, until the onions are softened. Stir in the cumin, oregano, paprika, mint, red pepper flakes, bulgur, and lentils. Stir and cook for 2 minutes to lightly cook the spices. Stir in the broth and tomatoes. Bring to a boil, then reduce the heat to simmer. Cook, stirring occasionally, for 30 minutes or until tender. Remove from the heat and stir in the lemon juice. Taste and adjust the seasonings.

Put the Swiss chard in a large skillet. Cook over medium heat for 3 minutes until bright green but not dry. Add a splash of water when cooking to keep it moist. Season the chard with salt and pepper.

To serve, ladle the soup between 4 bowls. Top each bowl with an equal amount of Swiss chard and pine nuts.

YIELD: 4 to 6 servings

Spicy Chickpea and Any Grain Soup

▶ **GRAIN**: CHOICE ▶ GLUTEN-FREE POTENTIAL ▶ SOY-FREE POTENTIAL

This is the ultimate in customizable soup. Some might call it "clean-out-the-fridge soup," but let's keep that secret. If you have beans that are waiting for a purpose, use those. No fire-roasted tomatoes? A can of diced or crushed will do the trick, too. I've tried many kinds of harissa and they all vary in heat; let me emphasize to cook to your own taste.

1 tablespoon (15 ml) olive oil

½ large onion, minced

1 carrot, peeled and diced

1 stalk celery, diced

1 small parsnip, peeled and diced

2 teaspoons (5 g) ground cumin

2 teaspoons (4 g) ground coriander

1 teaspoon smoked paprika

½ teaspoon dried thyme

4 to 6 cloves garlic, minced

¼ cup (60 ml) dry red wine, or additional water

6 cups (1.4 L) water

1 can (15 ounces, or 425 g) chickpeas, drained and rinsed

1 can (14.5 ounces, or 411 g) diced fire-roasted tomatoes, undrained

1 cup (weight varies) cooked barley, einkorn, freekeh, kamut, or quinoa

1 to 2 tablespoons (15 to 30 g) harissa (medium or hot), to taste

¼ teaspoon liquid smoke, optional, to taste

5 ounces (140 g) baby kale

Salt and pepper

Heat the oil in a large soup pot over medium heat. Add the onion, carrot, celery, and parsnip. Cook for 3 to 4 minutes until the onion is translucent. Add the cumin, coriander, paprika, thyme, and garlic. Cook, stirring occasionally, for 3 to 5 minutes, to toast the spices. Add the wine. Stir to deglaze the pot. Add the water, chickpeas, tomatoes, grain, harissa, and liquid smoke. Bring to a boil, then reduce to simmer for 20 minutes. Stir in the baby kale and for 3 to 4 minutes until wilted. Season to taste with salt and pepper.

YIELD: 4 to 6 servings

Albóndigas Soup

▶ **GRAIN**: BULGUR

Albóndigas: Fun to say, even better to eat. Our Mexican Wheatballs (page 91) are cooked in a light vegetable broth, seasoned with a roasted poblano pepper for extra oomph. The soup somehow manages to be elegant and rustic at the same time, making it ideal for nearly any situation.

1 tablespoon (15 ml) olive oil

1 cup (160 g) chopped onion

1 poblano pepper, roasted, peeled, seeded, and chopped

2 carrots, peeled and chopped

1 stalk celery, chopped

4 to 6 cloves garlic, minced

1 recipe Mexican Wheatballs (page 91)

1 can (14.5 ounces or 411 g) diced tomatoes

6 cups (1.4 L) water

2 vegan bouillon cubes

1 teaspoon chili powder, more to taste

1 teaspoon dried cilantro

1 teaspoon dried oregano

1 teaspoon dried thyme

Salt and pepper

Heat the oil, onion, poblano, carrots, celery, and garlic in a large soup pot over medium-high heat. Cook for 3 to 5 minutes, stirring occasionally, until fragrant. Add the wheatballs, tomatoes, water, bouillon, chili powder, cilantro, oregano, and thyme. Bring to a boil, then reduce to simmer for 30 minutes, stirring gently every once in a while. Season to taste with salt and pepper.

YIELD: 4 to 6 servings

Roasted Corn and Barley Chowder

▶ **GRAIN**: BARLEY (HULLED) ▶ SOY-FREE POTENTIAL

The perfect bowl of thick chowder to come home to when all you crave is healthy, flavorful, comfort food. We love the textural addition of barley here! We recommend using homemade, low- or no-sodium broth powder so as not to overwhelm the flavors.

1 yellow bell pepper, left whole

1 to 2 jalapeño peppers, trimmed, halved, and seeded, to taste

2½ cups (400 g) frozen sweet white or yellow corn

Slightly heaping ½ cup (90 g) raw cashews, soaked overnight (see page 166)

2¾ cups (650 ml) water, divided

2 tablespoons (16 g) Broth Powder (page 167)

1 tablespoon (10 g) minced garlic

¼ cup plus 3 tablespoons (40 g) chopped scallion (white and green parts)

¼ teaspoon fine sea salt, to taste

1 tablespoon (15 ml) fresh lime juice

1 tablespoon (15 ml) fresh lemon juice

1½ cups (236 g) cooked hulled barley (al dente)

Fresh herb of choice, lime or lemon wedges, for garnish

Preheat the oven to 425°F (220°C, or gas mark 7). Place all the peppers on a medium-rimmed baking sheet. Roast until soft and slightly charred, about 15 minutes for the jalapeño and 30 minutes for the bell pepper. Check every 5 to 10 minutes to make sure the peppers don't burn. When done, place the peppers in a glass bowl fitted with a lid to steam for about 10 minutes. Once cool enough to handle, peel the peppers. Discard their seeds and core.

At the same time, place the frozen corn in a 9-inch (23 cm) square baking pan, and roast until lightly browned for a total of about 25 minutes, stirring every 10 minutes.

Place the peppers, cashews, 1 cup (235 ml) water, broth powder, garlic, scallion, salt, lime juice, and lemon juice in a food processor or blender. Process until smooth, stopping to scrape sides occasionally. Transfer this mixture to a large pot with the roasted corn. Add the remaining 1¾ cups (415 ml) water. Bring to a low boil, cover with the lid and simmer 15 minutes. Add the cooked barley and simmer for another 5 minutes until heated through. Garnish as desired. If you foresee leftovers, we recommend keeping the barley and chowder separate. Add the grain as needed upon reheating to avoid mushy barley.

YIELD: 4 to 6 servings

Recipe Note

Peppers are often steamed in sandwich bags, which work well if the bags are sturdy enough. If they aren't, there is a potential risk of having the heat of the peppers melt the plastic. Not fun! That's why we're more partial to the bowl method these days.

Tempeh Lentil Soup with Freekeh

▶ **GRAIN**: CRACKED FREEKEH OR CHOICE

It's not often that we use prepared foods in our recipes, but with tempeh bacon, we make an exception. Here, the smoky undertone of the bacon is the ideal partner for the earthy lentils, while the cauliflower florets bring a lighter and brighter flavor. It's a bowl full of awesome.

1 tablespoon (15 ml) high heat neutral-flavored oil

1 package (6 ounces, or 170 g) tempeh bacon, chopped

½ medium onion, minced

1 large carrot, chopped

1 stalk celery, chopped

1 cup (100 g) small cauliflower florets

2 cloves garlic, minced

½ teaspoon dried basil

½ teaspoon dried thyme

¼ teaspoon dried rosemary

¼ teaspoon dried tarragon

¼ cup dry white wine, or additional water

½ cup (96 g) French green lentils

6 cups (1.4 L) water

2 teaspoons (12 g) vegan bouillon paste

1 tablespoon (15 ml) tamari

¼ teaspoon liquid smoke, optional

½ cup (116 g, weight varies) cooked cracked freekeh, einkorn, or barley

Salt and pepper

1 tablespoon (4 g) minced fresh parsley

Heat the oil in a large soup pot over medium-high heat. Add the tempeh bacon and cook for 4 to 6 minutes, stirring occasionally, until browned. Reduce the heat to medium. Add the onion through (and including) the tarragon. Stir and cook for 2 to 3 minutes until the garlic is fragrant. Add the wine, stirring to bring any bits off the bottom of the soup pot. Add the lentils, water, bouillon paste, tamari, and liquid smoke. Bring to a boil, then simmer for 30 to 35 minutes until the lentils are tender. Stir in the freekeh, and season to taste with salt and pepper. Stir in the parsley and serve.

YIELD: 4 to 6 servings

Italian Wedding Soup

▶ GRAIN: BULGUR

If you happen to plan ahead, the Italian Wheatballs (page 90) can be made half-size in exactly the same way. Or, live on the edge like we do. Use that spoon in your hand to break them apart to get the perfect bite in every spoonful.

1 tablespoon (15 ml) olive oil

1 large leek, white part only, cleaned, sliced in thin half-moons

1 stalk celery, sliced

2 large carrots, peeled and sliced

2 teaspoons (3 g) Italian seasoning blend

1 teaspoon dried oregano

½ teaspoon fine sea salt

Generous pinch ground white pepper

4 cloves garlic, minced

⅓ cup (80 ml) dry white wine, or additional water

1 recipe Italian Wheatballs (page 90)

2 tablespoons (15 g) nutritional yeast

1 handful sliced cabbage

8 cups (2 L) water

1 to 2 tablespoons (18 to 36 g) vegan bouillon paste

1 cup (168 g) dry orzo

2 packed cups (80 g) baby spinach, sliced

Black pepper

Heat the oil in a large soup pot over medium heat. Add the leek, celery, carrots, Italian seasoning, oregano, salt, white pepper, and garlic. Cook for 2 minutes, stirring occasionally, to coat the vegetables with oil. Add the wine, wheatballs, nutritional yeast, cabbage, water, and one-half of the bouillon paste. Bring to a boil, then reduce the heat to simmer. Simmer for 20 minutes. Add the orzo, spinach, and additional bouillon, if desired. Cook for 10 minutes longer or until the orzo is tender. Season to taste with black pepper.

YIELD: 6 servings

Recipe Note

If you do not plan to eat all the soup at once, cook the orzo separately and add it to the individual servings to avoid orzo bloat.

Minestrone with Teff

▶ GRAIN: TEFF ▶ SOY-FREE POTENTIAL

Minestrone soup has always been a favorite of ours, so adding a whole grain to it was a no-brainer. We opted for teff, which is barely noticeable, and you'll still get that whole-grain goodness in every bowl!

2 tablespoons (30 ml) olive oil

1 cup (160 g) chopped onion

2 carrots, peeled and chopped

1 stalk celery, chopped

1 small zucchini, chopped

4 to 6 cloves garlic, minced

1 teaspoon dried basil

1 teaspoon dried oregano

½ teaspoon dried thyme

Pinch red pepper flakes

1 bay leaf

½ cup (120 ml) dry red wine, or additional water

1 can (14.5 ounces, or 411 g) crushed fire-roasted tomatoes

1 can (14.5 ounces, or 411 g) diced tomatoes

1 vegan bouillon cube

5 cups (1.2 L) water

½ cup (100 g) dry teff

½ cup (60 g) green beans 1-inch (2.5 cm) pieces

1 cup (112 g) cooked small pasta, such as cavatelli

Salt and pepper

Minced fresh basil or parsley, for garnish

Heat the oil in a large soup pot over medium heat. Add the onion. Cook for 3 minutes until softened. Add the carrots, celery, zucchini, garlic, basil, oregano, thyme, red pepper flakes, and bay leaf. Cook and stir for 3 to 4 minutes until fragrant. Add the red wine, tomatoes, bouillon, water, and teff. Bring to a boil, then reduce the heat to simmer and cook for 20 minutes. The teff will want to stick to the bottom of the pot, so stir it occasionally. Add the green beans and cook for 10 minutes. Add the pasta, stir to combine. Remove the bay leaf. Taste and adjust the seasonings. Garnish with the fresh basil or parsley when serving.

YIELD: 4 to 6 servings

Pozole Verde with Farro

▶ **GRAIN**: FARRO ▶ SOY-FREE POTENTIAL

Eat your greens! In the form of a delightfully hearty and spicy Mexican soup, that is. The wide array of potential garnishes makes the *pozole* even more fun to enjoy.

1 cup (208 g) dry farro, rinsed and drained

2½ cups (590 ml) vegetable broth

1 to 2 medium jalapeño peppers, trimmed, seeded, and quartered, to taste

1 to 2 poblano peppers, trimmed, seeded, and quartered, to taste

4 medium tomatillos, skinned and quartered

½ cup plus 2 tablespoons (60 g) chopped scallion

¾ cup (12 g) fresh cilantro leaves

1½ tablespoons (15 g) chopped garlic

¾ teaspoon coarse kosher salt, divided

1 generous teaspoon dried oregano leaves

Ground black pepper, to taste

1 (25-ounce, or 708 g) can white hominy, rinsed and drained

4 cups (940 ml) water

2 tablespoons (16 g) Broth Powder (page 167)

GARNISHES:

Sliced red radish, lime wedges, diced avocado tossed with fresh lime juice, for garnish

Toasted cumin seeds, for garnish, optional

Tortilla chips or toasted pepitas (hulled pumpkin seeds), for garnish, optional

Place the farro in a rice cooker or large pot. Cover with broth and stir to combine. Follow the manufacturer's instructions if using a rice cooker. Bring to a boil if cooking on the stove. Cover with a lid, lower the temperature and simmer until al dente, about 20 to 25 minutes. Drain, if needed, and set aside.

In a large food processor, place the peppers, tomatillos, scallions, cilantro, garlic, ½ teaspoon salt, oregano, and pepper. Once completely smooth, transfer to a large pot. Cook on medium heat, stirring occasionally, until dark green, about 10 minutes.

Place the hominy, remaining ¼ teaspoon salt, water, and broth powder on top of the green sauce, stirring to combine. Bring to a low boil, lower the heat and simmer partially covered for 15 minutes. Portion out the cooked farro in bowls, ladle the pozole on top, and garnish as desired. Leftovers of farro and pozole can be stored separately in airtight containers in the refrigerator for up to 4 days.

YIELD: 6 servings

Recipe Notes

- You can choose any grain you want to use here, simply adjust both cooking time and method to what you pick. We prefer adding the cooked grain to the individual servings so that it doesn't lose its texture.

- While cilantro clearly works perfectly with the other flavors here, we understand not everyone is a fan. You could always replace it with fresh parsley, if you really must.

Onion, Leek, and Grain Soup

▶ GRAIN: ANY

It might not be quite as common in the United States, but Celine has memories of onion soup being a popular item served at many social events back in Switzerland. Here's an easy vegan version, made even heartier and more rustic thanks to the addition of whole grains.

1 tablespoon (15 ml) grapeseed or olive oil

1 large yellow onion, chopped

6 ounces (170 g) chopped leek (thoroughly cleaned and drained, see Recipe Note)

2 teaspoons (13 g) agave nectar, optional

2 large cloves garlic, minced

½ teaspoon caraway seeds

½ teaspoon coarse kosher salt, to taste

Ground black peppercorn, to taste

2 large sprigs fresh thyme

2 tablespoons (16 g) Broth Powder (page 167)

4 cups (940 ml) water

1½ cups (approximately 280 g) cooked spelt berries, kamut, einkorn, wheat berries, triticale berries, or wild rice

Splash of dry vegan white wine (2 tablespoons, or 30 ml), to taste, optional

1 prepared recipe Slightly Cheesy Cashew Sauce (page 166), to taste

Heat the oil in a large pot. Add the onion and leek. Cook on medium-high heat until browned, stirring occasionally and adjusting the heat to prevent burning, about 10 minutes. If the onion and leek are slow to brown, add the agave to help move things along before the veggies get too mushy. Add the garlic and sauté another minute. Add the caraway seeds, salt, pepper, thyme, broth powder, and water. Partially cover with a lid and simmer 10 minutes. Add the cooked grain and a splash of wine, simmer another 10 minutes. Discard the thyme sprigs.

Serve portions of soup in oven-safe bowls, top with a generous spoonful of cashew sauce, and broil a few minutes to brown the sauce. Keep an eye on it, though, so it doesn't burn.

YIELD: 4 to 6 servings

Recipe Note

It's easier to brown the onion and leek if the leek is thoroughly drained from its cleaning water, otherwise it will steam before it browns. Consider spinning it dry for best results, if time allows.

Roasted Corn and Sorghum Salad with Chipotle Dressing

▶ **GRAIN:** SORGHUM ▶ GLUTEN-FREE POTENTIAL ▶ SOY-FREE POTENTIAL

It took us quite a few attempts to master sorghum as we find it is a little more finicky to work with than other grains. Soaking it overnight and cooking it to perfect tenderness is key. Once you get these steps, we're sure you will love it, too. We're especially fond of it in this summery, colorful salad. If you have a hard time locating sorghum, hulled barley or brown rice would be good substitutes.

FOR THE DRESSING:

½ cup (120 g) Basic Cashew Cream (page 166)

¾ teaspoon agave nectar

¾ teaspoon canned chipotle pepper in adobo

½ teaspoon adobo sauce

Generous ⅛ teaspoon ground cumin

¼ cup (3 g) very loosely packed, chopped fresh cilantro

1 tablespoon (15 ml) fresh lime juice

1 small clove garlic, grated or pressed

Salt, to taste

FOR THE SALAD:

Scant 2¼ cups (360 g) frozen sweet white corn

1 teaspoon agave nectar

1½ cups (248 g) cooked sorghum

5 tablespoons (30 g) chopped scallion (white and green parts)

8 ounces (227 g) mini heirloom tomatoes, quartered or halved depending on size

To make the dressing: Place the cashew cream, agave, chipotle pepper, adobo sauce, cumin, cilantro, lime juice, garlic, and salt in a small blender or use an immersion blender. Blend until perfectly smooth. Store in an airtight jar in the refrigerator until ready to use.

To make the salad: Preheat the oven to 425°F (220°C, or gas mark 7). Place the frozen corn in a 9-inch (23 cm) square baking pan and roast 10 minutes. Add the agave, stirring carefully to combine, and roast for another 10 minutes. Stir again. Finish roasting for another 5 minutes until quite a few of the grains are lightly browned. Remove from the oven and set aside.

Heat the sorghum in a skillet over medium-high heat for 2 minutes while stirring occasionally until heated through. Turn off the heat, but leave the skillet on the stove. Add the chopped scallion and tomatoes, stir to combine. Let stand for a couple of minutes, to soften slightly and let the flavors meld. Stir the corn into the sorghum and tomatoes. Adjust seasoning, if desired. Drizzle dressing to taste over each serving.

YIELD: 4 servings, ½ cup (120 ml) dressing

Rye and Sauerkraut Salad

▶ GRAIN: RYE BERRIES ▶ SOY-FREE POTENTIAL

Tami's mom used to make a sauerkraut salad, so Tami couldn't resist pairing kraut with rye for an updated version. This is an ideal side dish and a unique potluck dish that is sure to spark conversation. The recipe is easily tripled or quadrupled to feed a crowd.

½ cup (90 g) dry rye berries

1 cup (112 g) sauerkraut, drained

½ cup (80 g) minced onion

½ cup (75 g) minced red bell pepper

½ cup (120 g) minced celery

½ teaspoon brown mustard seeds

¼ teaspoon celery seeds

¼ teaspoon ground black pepper

⅓ cup (80 ml) apple cider vinegar

⅓ cup (60 g) evaporated cane juice

1 teaspoon Dijon mustard

Salt and pepper

Put the rye berries in a medium-size saucepan and cover with 3 to 4 inches (7.5 to 10 cm) of water. Bring to a boil, cover, and reduce the heat to simmer. Cook for 50 minutes or until tender. Drain and run under cold water. Transfer to a medium-size bowl. Add the sauerkraut, onion, bell pepper, celery, mustard seeds, celery seeds, and black pepper.

Heat the vinegar, evaporated cane juice, and mustard in a small saucepan over medium-high heat. Stir and cook until the evaporated cane juice is dissolved. Pour over the rye mixture and stir to coat. Cover and refrigerate for 30 minutes for the flavors to blend. The salad can be refrigerated airtight for up to 3 days. Taste and adjust the seasonings when serving.

YIELD: 1 pound (454 g) salad

Recipe Note

If you can get local sauerkraut with live enzymes, it's the best! If not, Bubbies is a favorite of ours. Look for it in the refrigerated section of your grocery store.

Quinoa Tabbouleh

▶ **GRAIN**: QUINOA ▶ GLUTEN-FREE POTENTIAL ▶ SOY-FREE POTENTIAL

Sometimes, we're all about fancy dishes that take quite a bit of time to prepare, but we're also into supereasy food that takes moments to go from prep to eating. This is one of those recipes where everything comes together in no time (provided the quinoa is at the ready in the refrigerator) with outstanding results to boot. Granted, it's hard to go wrong whenever quinoa is involved!

2 tablespoons (30 ml) fresh lemon juice

2 tablespoons (30 ml) grapeseed oil or extra-virgin olive oil

1 ounce (28 g) minced shallot (about 1 medium)

½ cup (30 g) chopped fresh parsley leaves

¼ cup (40 g) sulfur-free, organic, dried Turkish apricots, minced

¼ teaspoon ground cinnamon

¼ teaspoon ground allspice

2 cups (370 g) cooked and cooled quinoa

½ cup (80 g) cooked chickpeas

1 to 2 cloves garlic, minced, to taste

½ teaspoon coarse kosher salt, to taste

Cayenne pepper, red pepper flakes, or ground black pepper, to taste

¼ cup (27 g) toasted slivered almonds, optional

Fold all the ingredients in a large bowl and cover with a lid. Let stand for at least 30 minutes before serving to let the flavors meld. Store leftovers in an airtight container in the refrigerator for up to 2 days.

YIELD: 4 servings

Recipe Notes

- Serve this tabbouleh meze–style with lightly dressed cucumber or carrot salad, and with our Zhoug Farro Falafel (page 93) or Cracked Wheat Koftas (page 88) while you're at it!

- We're not trying to be posh and picky with the kind of dried apricot to use in this dish: If you've ever tried the ones listed here, you already know how amazing they taste. Far softer than other sulfur-free apricots, healthier than the sulfured kind . . . we cannot recommend them enough!

Za'atar Shirazi Oat Salad

▶ **GRAIN**: OAT GROATS ▶ GLUTEN-FREE POTENTIAL ▶ SOY-FREE POTENTIAL

Za'atar is a Middle Eastern spice blend composed of herbs, sumac, and sesame seeds. Shirazi is a Persian side salad that traditionally includes fresh tomatoes, cucumber, and onion. Combine both concepts, along with some oat groats cooked to pilaf texture, and you get a super summer-friendly salad. Make this salad the night before, store in mason jars, and take it to work the next day for a perfect refreshing, healthy, and filling lunch—if you can wait that long.

1 cup (184 g) dry oat groats, rinsed and drained

3 cups (705 ml) vegetable broth

1 teaspoon dried oregano or thyme leaves

1 teaspoon ground sumac

1 teaspoon toasted cumin seeds

¼ teaspoon coarse kosher salt, plus extra to taste

1 teaspoon toasted sesame seeds

1½ tablespoons (23 ml) fresh lime juice

1½ tablespoons (23 ml) white balsamic vinegar

1½ tablespoons (23 ml) grapeseed or extra-virgin olive oil

1 large clove garlic, grated or pressed

8 ounces (227 g) mini heirloom tomatoes of various colors, diced

2 Persian cucumbers, diced

¼ cup (40 g) minced red onion

Ground black pepper, to taste

Handful chopped pistachios, to taste, optional

Combine the oat groats and broth in a large pot. Bring to a boil, partially cover, and simmer 30 minutes or until just al dente. Check occasionally and do not overcook. The grains must be pilaf-like not porridge-like. Drain the extra liquid, if needed. Set aside to cool.

Prepare the za'atar by placing the oregano, sumac, cumin seeds, and salt in a mortar. Gently crush with a pestle. Stir the sesame seeds into the blend.

Combine the lime juice, vinegar, oil, and garlic in a medium bowl. Stir the cooked oats, tomatoes, cucumber, and onion into the vinaigrette. Add the following to taste: za'atar blend, salt, and pepper. We usually start with 2½ teaspoons (7 g) za'atar, and go from there. Let stand 1 hour before serving. When ready to serve, garnish each portion with pistachios. You can always add extra za'atar upon eating. Store leftover za'atar in an airtight spice jar for up to 1 month.

YIELD: 4 side-dish servings, about 1½ tablespoons (12 g) za'atar blend

Roasted Vegetable Einkorn Salad

▸ **GRAIN**: EINKORN ▸ SOY-FREE POTENTIAL

The roasted vegetables have deep, earthy undertones, that are perfectly balanced with a red pepper and balsamic dressing. Your baking times will vary based on the size of your asparagus and the size you cut the other vegetables. Check them every 5 minutes or so after the first 15 minutes have passed.

FOR THE SALAD:

10 stalks asparagus, trimmed

1 cup (100 g) small cauliflower florets

½ red bell pepper, cut into ½-inch (1.3 cm) thick slices

½ cup (62 g) chopped zucchini

2 (½-inch or 1.3 cm) thick half-moon onion slices

1 tablespoon (15 ml) olive oil

Salt and pepper

1½ cups (192 g) prepared einkorn, cooled

FOR THE DRESSING:

¼ cup (45 g) jarred roasted red pepper, rinsed and chopped

1 clove garlic

2 tablespoons (30 ml) balsamic vinegar

2 tablespoons (30 ml) vegetable broth

½ teaspoon salt

¼ teaspoon ground black pepper

To make the salad: Heat the oven to 400 °F (200°C, or gas mark 6). Pour the oil into a medium-size bowl. Add the asparagus and toss to coat, then transfer to one end of a 9 x 13-inch (23 x 33 cm) baking pan. Continue with the cauliflower, bell pepper, zucchini, and onions, covering each with oil. Season with salt and pepper. Start checking the vegetables at 15 minutes, removing those that are roasted and returning the others to the oven. When the asparagus, bell pepper, and onions are done, chop them into ½-inch (1.3 cm) pieces. Let the vegetables cool, then transfer them to medium-size bowl. Add the einkorn.

To make the dressing: Combine all the ingredients in a small blender and process until completely smooth. Pour over the salad and toss to coat. Let sit at least 30 minutes for the flavors to meld, or cover and refrigerate. Let the salad come to room temperature before serving.

YIELD: 4 to 6 servings

Kamut-bouli

▶ GRAIN: KAMUT ▶ SOY-FREE POTENTIAL

This recipe is our favorite version, and we'd love for you to make it yours! Feel free to swap out the vegetables for whatever you prefer, or just add to it. Are your cherry tomatoes at their best? Add more. For a salty addition, add some quartered olives. Are you a big fan of mint? Double that amount. Basil not your thing? *(Who are you?)* Feel free to leave it out. This one is made to customize.

1 cup (184 g) dry kamut

1 cup (104 g) minced cucumber

¾ cup (112 g) minced bell pepper

¼ cup plus 2 tablespoons (60 g) minced scallions

20 cherry tomatoes, quartered

¼ cup (16 g) minced fresh parsley

2 tablespoons (8 g) minced fresh basil

1 tablespoon (4 g) minced fresh mint, optional

¼ cup (60 ml) fresh lemon juice

2 tablespoons (30 ml) olive oil

2 cloves garlic, minced

Salt and pepper

Prepare kamut according to package directions. Drain and run under cold water. Put the kamut in a medium-size bowl, and add the remaining ingredients. Stir to combine, and season to taste. Cover and refrigerate for 30 minutes for the flavors to meld. Season to taste when serving.

YIELD: 4 servings

Einkorn Kale Salad with Apricots

▶ **GRAIN:** EINKORN, BARLEY, CRACKED OR WHOLE FREEKEH

Mmmm . . . kale! It's the green that knows its place so well. And that place is any-where and everywhere! Kale, vegetables, and einkorn are joined by sweet bits of dried apricot, crunchy sunflower seeds, and a full-flavor miso dressing to create a supersatisfying salad. Oh, and that's a no-oil-added salad dressing. Bonus!

8 ounces (227 g) kale, chopped

1½ cups (227 g) prepared einkorn, barley, or freekeh, drained and cooled

½ cup (50 g) small cauliflower florets

1 carrot, peeled and grated

¼ cup (33 g) minced dried apricots

¼ cup (60 ml) vegetable broth

1 tablespoon (15 ml) white wine vinegar

2 tablespoons (15 g) nutritional yeast

2 tablespoons (36 g) red miso

1 tablespoon (9 g) salted, roasted sunflower seeds (see Recipe Note)

Salt and pepper

Put the kale in a medium-size bowl and rub it with your hands to break it down some, for 4 to 6 minutes, or to desired texture. Stir in the einkorn, cauliflower, carrot, and apricots.

Combine the broth, vinegar, nutritional yeast, and miso in a small blender. Process until smooth. Pour over the kale and einkorn mixture. Stir to coat. Season to taste with salt and pepper, and stir in the sunflower seeds when serving.

YIELD: 2 servings

Recipe Note

If you tend to be a little salt sensitive, substitute un-salted, roasted sunflower seeds for the salted ones.

Tex-Mex Freekeh Salad

▶ GRAIN: FREEKEH

We think of this as an updated, more whole-grain version of a taco salad. If you see it like we do, feel free to add your favorites to the salad, such as sliced black olives or, even better, roasted corn cut from the cob.

2 cups (approximately 336 g) prepared whole freekeh, or quinoa, or barley, cooled

2 cups (344 g) cooked black beans

1½ cups (135 g) chopped cabbage

1 head romaine lettuce, chopped

½ cup (75 g) chopped red bell pepper

¼ cup (28 g) chopped carrots

¼ cup (40 g) minced scallion

1 tablespoon (9 g) minced poblano, or to taste

½ cup (75 g) favorite red salsa (we like medium or hot)

1 roasted red bell pepper (jarred), rinsed

1 chipotle in adobo, optional, more to taste

1 tablespoon (15 ml) red wine vinegar, optional

Salt and pepper

1 avocado, pitted, peeled, and chopped

Combine the freekeh, beans, cabbage, romaine, bell pepper, carrots, scallion, and poblano in a large bowl. Combine the salsa, roasted red bell pepper, and chipotle in a small blender. Process until smooth. Taste and add the red wine vinegar, if more tang is needed. It depends on the salsa. Process again. Pour over the salad, and stir to combine. Taste and adjust the seasonings. Gently stir in the avocado.

YIELD: 4 servings

Freekeh Fritters

▶ **GRAIN**: WHOLE FREEKEH ▶ SOY-FREE POTENTIAL ▶ QUICK AND EASY

Fritters are fun foods and they are, admittedly, slightly indulgent because they are fried. They aren't an everyday thing, but when they are a "today!" treat we do it right! Freekeh and corn make an incredibly tasty (and slightly healthier) fritter: That's our story, and we're sticking to it. For a quick dipping sauce, stir together vegan sour cream and salsa to taste. Or try these fritters with a harissa and lemon juice–spiked mayo for an incredible snack.

¾ cup (180 ml) plain vegan milk

1 cup (164 g) frozen corn kernels, thawed and divided

1 clove garlic, peeled

1 cup (approximately 168 g) cooked and cooled whole freekeh, barley, or einkorn

⅓ cup (50 g) minced red onion

½ teaspoon ground coriander

½ teaspoon fine sea salt

¼ teaspoon ground black pepper

1½ cups (186 g) all-purpose flour, divided

High heat neutral-flavored oil, for cooking

Combine the milk, ½ cup (68 g) corn, and garlic in small blender. Process until smooth. Pour into a medium-size bowl. Add the freekeh, onion, coriander, salt, and pepper. Stir to combine. Add 1 cup (124 g) flour to form a thick batter. Put the remaining flour on a plate. Scoop a rounded tablespoon (30 g) of fritter batter and drop it in the flour on the plate. Pat it into a small disk, no more than ½-inch (1.3 cm) thick and coat with flour. Repeat until all fritters are formed. Heat a thin layer of oil in large skillet over medium-high heat. Cook the fritters in batches, for 3 to 5 minutes until browned. Turn and cook the second side, about 3 to 5 minutes. Transfer to a plate lined with a paper towel.

YIELD: 16 to 20 fritters

Freekeh Fritters and Kale Salad

▶ **GRAIN:** WHOLE FREEKEH

Warm, whole-grain fritters top a perfectly dressed salad. How perfect? Well, when you make this zesty dressing to taste, you just know it can't be beat. Roasted asparagus is always a welcome addition to any meal, and here we pair it with the optional (slightly sweet) roasted parsnip and oh-so-green baby kale.

FOR THE SALAD AND FRITTERS:

6 to 8 stalks asparagus, trimmed and cut into 1-inch (2.5 cm) pieces

1 parsnip, peeled and cut into ½-inch (1.3 cm) slices, optional

2 teaspoons olive oil, divided

5 ounces (140 g) baby kale

Few slices red onion, halved or quartered

Handful cherry tomatoes, halved

½ bell pepper, chopped (any color)

1 recipe Freekeh Fritters, prepared (page 158)

FOR THE DRESSING:

3 tablespoons (45 ml) vegetable broth

1 tablespoon (16 g) tahini paste

1 tablespoon (15 ml) seasoned rice vinegar

1 tablespoon (15 ml) fresh lemon juice

1 tablespoon (18 g) light miso (such as South River Sweet Brown Rice Miso)

2 teaspoons harissa, or to taste

1 clove garlic, peeled

½ teaspoon toasted sesame oil

Salt and pepper

Preheat the oven to 400°F (200°C, or gas mark 6).

To prepare the salad: In separate bowls, toss the asparagus and parsnip with 1 teaspoon oil each and season with salt and pepper. Put on opposite ends of a rimmed baking sheet. Bake the asparagus for 10 minutes or until tender, and transfer to a plate to cool. Bake the parsnips for 15 minutes or until tender, and transfer to the same plate. When cool, toss the asparagus, parsnip, and all remaining salad ingredients in a large bowl.

To prepare the dressing: Combine all the ingredients, except the salt and pepper, in a small blender. Process until smooth. Season to taste with additional harissa and salt and pepper.

To serve, pour the dressing over the salad and toss to coat. Divide the salad evenly among 4 plates. Top with one-quarter of the fritters and serve.

YIELD: 4 servings

Barley Edamame Salad

▶ **GRAIN**: BARLEY (HULLED)

Simplicity at its best: bold flavors, quick and easy preparation, and a handsome outcome. We really love using barley here. If you prefer to be a bit more traditional, switch to your favorite type of brown rice instead. Adjust cooking time and method accordingly.

1 cup (184 g) dry hulled barley, rinsed and drained

3 cups (705 ml) water

1 tablespoon (8 g) Broth Powder (page 167)

2 tablespoons (30 ml) toasted sesame oil

2 tablespoons (30 ml) seasoned rice vinegar

1½ tablespoons (23 ml) fresh lime juice

1 tablespoon (15 ml) tamari, more if needed

¼ to ½ teaspoon red pepper flakes, to taste

1 to 2 cloves garlic, grated or pressed, to taste

1 to 2 teaspoons (2 to 4 g) freshly grated ginger, to taste

9 ounces (255 g, approximately 1½ cups) shelled ready-to-eat edamame, rinsed and drained

¼ cup (20 g) minced scallion

Black sesame seeds or toasted regular sesame seeds, to taste

Place the barley in a rice cooker or large pot. Cover with water and broth powder, stir to combine. Follow the manufacturer's instructions if using a rice cooker. Bring to a boil if cooking on the stove. Cover with a lid, lower the temperature, and simmer until al dente, 30 to 40 minutes. Check for doneness occasionally, and either drain early or add extra liquid (if needed) to extend the cooking time. You can prepare the barley the night before and refrigerate it overnight.

In a large bowl, whisk to combine the oil, vinegar, lime juice, tamari, red pepper flakes, garlic, and ginger. Add the barley, edamame, and scallion, and fold to thoroughly coat. Add extra tamari, if desired. Add a sprinkle of sesame seeds on top of each serving. Leftovers can be stored in an airtight container in the refrigerator for up to 3 days. Fold again to combine before serving.

YIELD: 4 to 6 servings

Wheat Berry Mechwia

▶ **GRAIN**: WHEAT BERRIES

Mechwia is a flavor-packed Tunisian salad composed of roasted vegetables, briny capers, and olives. It also usually showcases eggs and tuna. We've kept the best parts of the original and added wheat berries. We chose not to roast the tomatoes, using flavor-packed, beautiful, ripe, heirloom tomatoes instead. Serve with Zhoug Farro Falafel (page 93) or Cracked Wheat Koftas (page 88). Kamut, spelt, triticale berries, or any similar grain can be subbed for the wheat berries. Adjust cooking times accordingly.

¾ cup (144 g) dry, soft, white wheat berries, rinsed and drained

1 tablespoon (8 g) Broth Powder (page 167)

1 whole green bell pepper

1 whole jalapeño pepper

½ red onion, peeled and halved

3 whole cloves garlic, peeled

2 large ripe heirloom tomatoes, chopped

12 kalamata and green olives (a mix of both), pitted and chopped

1½ tablespoons (23 ml) capers with brine, coarsely minced

1 tablespoon (15 ml) extra-virgin olive oil

1 tablespoon (15 ml) fresh lemon juice

½ teaspoon ground sumac

½ teaspoon ground cumin

Salt, to taste

Chopped fresh parsley or mint, for garnish

Place the wheat berries in a pot, cover with an extra 3 inches (7.5 cm) of water and 1 tablespoon (8 g) broth powder. Bring to a boil. Partially cover with a lid, lower the heat, and simmer until tender, about 1 hour. Drain, if needed, and set aside.

Preheat the oven to 425°F (220°C, or gas mark 7). Place peppers, onion, and garlic on a lightly greased, medium rimmed baking sheet and place in oven. Roasting times will vary; about 30 minutes for bell pepper (must be soft and charred) and onion (must be softer and browned), 15 minutes for the jalapeño (must be soft and charred) and garlic (must be soft and browned). Check every 5 to 10 minutes to prevent burning, and flip halfway through. When ready, place the peppers in a glass bowl fitted with a lid for 10 minutes. Once cool enough to handle, peel the peppers. Discard the seeds and core. Mince the garlic, and chop or thinly slice the peppers and onion.

Place the wheat berries, tomatoes, peppers, onion, garlic, olives, capers, oil, lemon juice, sumac, and cumin in a large skillet. Fold to combine and cook on low heat for 4 minutes, just to meld the flavors. Adjust seasoning, if needed, and garnish with parsley or mint. Gently reheated leftovers are even better!

YIELD: 4 side-dish servings

Warm Farro and Sweet Potato Salad

▶ **GRAIN**: FARRO ▶ SOY-FREE POTENTIAL

Hello, versatility: Any favorite grain can be used in place of *fantastico* farro in this energy-packed, autumnal salad.

FOR THE DRESSING:

1¼ cups (228 g) cooked cannellini beans

3 tablespoons (45 ml) grapeseed or olive oil

3 tablespoons (45 ml) water

3 tablespoons (45 ml) fresh lemon juice

1 to 3 tablespoons (15 to 45 ml) apple cider vinegar, to taste

1 to 2 grated or pressed cloves garlic, to taste

1 tablespoon (3 g) packed minced fresh chives

½ teaspoon coarse kosher salt, to taste

1½ teaspoons Broth Powder (page 167)

Ground black pepper, to taste

FOR THE SALAD:

½ cup (100 g) dry farro, rinsed and drained

1 cup (235 ml) water

1½ tablespoons (12 g) Broth Powder (page 167), divided

1 pound (454 g) sweet potato, trimmed and chopped into bite-size pieces (about 2 medium)

½ cup plus 2 tablespoons (100 g) chopped shallot

½ teaspoon coarse kosher salt, to taste

½ teaspoon smoked paprika

¼ teaspoon ground cumin

Water, as needed

1½ cups (60 g) packed minced kale leaves

To make the dressing: Combine all ingredients in a blender, and blend until perfectly smooth. Adjust the vinegar to your liking. This can be made ahead of time and stored in an airtight container in the refrigerator for up to 3 days.

To make the salad: Place the farro, water, and 1 tablespoon (8 g) broth powder in a medium pot. Bring to a boil, lower the heat, and cover with a lid. Simmer until al dente, about 20 to 25 minutes. Drain early or add extra liquid (if needed) to reach desired texture. Set aside.

Place potato, shallot, salt, paprika, cumin, remaining 1½ teaspoons broth powder, and 1 tablespoon (15 ml) water in a large skillet. Cook on medium-high heat until the shallot is translucent, stirring occasionally. Add extra water, if needed. Lower the heat, cover with a lid, and cook until the potato is still firm, yet tender to the fork, about 10 minutes. Remove from the heat. Fold the kale and farro into the mixture. Heat the dressing slowly on low heat in a small saucepan until heated through, about 8 minutes, and drizzle as needed over the salad. Alternatively, add as much as you wish in the pan with the veggies and simmer until heated through.

YIELD: 4 servings, 1½ cups (355 ml) dressing

6

SPECTACULAR STAPLES FOR KITCHEN EASE

**A few, indispensable, not-so-little tricks
to boost flavors and round out dishes.**

While some of these recipes first appeared in other published books of ours, we felt they were too good to improve upon and added them here as a bonus for your viewing (and tasting) pleasure. We're quite positive they will become staples in your pantry, refrigerator, or freezer.

Basic Cashew Cream

▸ GLUTEN-FREE POTENTIAL
▸ SOY-FREE POTENTIAL

We turn to cashew cream as a substitute for soy yogurt in dipping sauces, or anywhere something creamy and rich is called for. For a slightly thicker cream, use only ¾ cup (180 ml) water. For a slightly less tangy cream, use 2 teaspoons (10 ml) fresh lemon juice.

1 cup (140 g) raw cashews, soaked overnight (see Recipe Note)

1 cup (235 ml) water

1 tablespoon (15 ml) fresh lemon juice

Pinch coarse kosher salt, to taste

Place the rinsed cashews in a blender along with water, lemon juice, and salt. Blend until completely smooth, stopping to scrape the sides occasionally. Transfer to a jar or airtight container. Cover tightly with plastic wrap or lid. Let stand at room temperature for 6 hours or until the cream smells slightly tangy. Store in an airtight container in the refrigerator for at least 2 days. The longer the cream sits, the tangier and thicker it gets. The cream will last for up to 2 weeks if stored properly in the refrigerator.

YIELD: 1⅓ cups (320 g)

Slightly Cheesy Cashew Sauce

▸ GLUTEN-FREE POTENTIAL

A sauce so perfectly flavored and decadent, no one will waste a nano-second missing cheese.

1 cup (140 g) raw cashews, soaked overnight (see Recipe Note)

1¼ cups (295 ml) vegetable broth

2 tablespoons (15 g) nutritional yeast

2 tablespoons (30 ml) fresh lemon juice

1 tablespoon (18 g) white miso

1 scant tablespoon (6 g) organic cornstarch

1 teaspoon onion powder

Fine sea salt

Place the rinsed cashews in a blender along with the broth, nutritional yeast, lemon juice, miso, cornstarch, onion powder, and salt to taste. Blend until completely smooth. Transfer to a small saucepot. Cook for approximately 8 minutes on medium heat, whisking frequently until thickened like fondue. Remove from the heat and whisk occasionally. Use immediately, or let cool and place in an airtight container in the refrigerator for up to 4 days. Slowly reheat in a saucepot before use.

YIELD: 2 cups (484 g)

Recipe Note

To soak cashews: Place cashews in a medium bowl or 4-cup (940 ml) glass measuring cup. Cover with 2 cups (470 ml) water. Cover with plastic wrap or a lid. Let stand at room temperature overnight (about 8 hours), to soften the nuts. Drain the cashews (discard soaking water), and give them a quick rinse. Proceed with recipe directions.

Broth Powder

▶ GLUTEN-FREE POTENTIAL ▶ SOY-FREE POTENTIAL ▶ QUICK AND EASY

If using another homemade broth powder in our recipes, you're missing out on something great. Just make sure it contains no salt or that it is low-sodium, so as not to overwhelm the dish. If your herbes de Provence mix contains lavender or fennel, it's best to steer clear and use Italian seasoning instead. Note: A slightly different version of this recipe originally appeared in *The Complete Guide to Even More Vegan Food Substitutions* (Newman and Steen, Fair Winds Press, 2015), and is included here for convenience.

1 ounce (28 g) sliced dried mushroom of choice (we love shiitake here)

1½ cups (180 g) nutritional yeast

2 tablespoons (15 g) onion powder

1 tablespoon (8 g) dried garlic powder

1 tablespoon (18 g) fine sea salt

1½ tablespoons (2 g) dried parsley, optional

1 tablespoon (7 g) smoked or regular paprika

1 tablespoon (3 g) dried oregano leaves (not powder, use only 1 teaspoon if powder)

1 tablespoon (4 g) herbes de Provence or Italian seasoning

1 teaspoon red pepper flakes, optional

1 teaspoon ground black pepper, to taste

Place all ingredients in a food processor. Process until thoroughly combined. It's okay if a few pieces of mushrooms are left slightly larger than the rest. Store in an airtight container at room temperature for up to 1 month. To prepare as 1 cup (235 ml) of broth, add 1 teaspoon (for lighter broth) or up to 1 tablespoon (for strongly flavored broth) (3 to 8 g) of the mix per 1 cup (235 ml) of water, depending on personal taste and use.

YIELD: 1¾ cups (245 g)

Kind-to-Cows Seitan

Our seitan recipes have loads of protein and they taste amazing, too! We keep cutlets in the freezer, thaw, and grill (or panfry) them for a quick dinner. Yes, really, they have enough flavor to serve without a sauce. They are also sensational used in any recipe. Note: These seitan recipes originally appeared in *The Great Vegan Protein Book* (Steen and Noyes, Fair Winds Press, 2015), and are included here for your convenience.

FOR THE SEITAN:

1¼ cups (180 g) vital wheat gluten

3 tablespoons (24 g) chickpea flour

1 tablespoon (12 g) granulated tapioca, such as Let's Do Organic

1 tablespoon (7 g) onion powder

1 teaspoon garlic powder

½ teaspoon ground black pepper

¾ cup (180 ml) vegetable broth, more if needed

1 tablespoon (15 g) organic ketchup

2 teaspoons (12 g) vegan bouillon paste

1 tablespoon (15 ml) high heat neutral-flavored oil, for cooking

FOR THE COOKING BROTH:

2 cups (470 ml) vegetable broth

1 tablespoon (15 g) organic ketchup

1 tablespoon (15 ml) tamari

1 teaspoon liquid smoke

¼ teaspoon ground black pepper

1 teaspoon toasted sesame oil

Preheat the oven to 300°F (150°C, or gas mark 3).

To make either seitan: Stir the dry ingredients together in a medium-size bowl. Stir the wet ingredients together in a measuring cup. Pour the wet ingredients into the dry ingredients and stir to combine. Knead with your hands to form a cohesive ball. Add an additional tablespoon gluten (9 g) or broth (15 ml), if needed, to reach the desired consistency. Divide into 6 equal portions. Sandwich a portion of dough between two pieces of parchment paper. Roll each portion into a cutlet that is no more than ½-inch (1.3 cm) thick. Heat the oil in a large skillet over medium-high heat. Cook the cutlets in batches, 3 to 5 minutes, until browned. Turn to cook the second side for 3 minutes until browned.

To prepare the cooking broth: Stir all the ingredients together in a 9 x 13 inch (22 x 23 cm) baking dish. Put the cutlets in the broth and cover the pan tightly with foil. Bake for 1 hour. Turn off the oven and let the seitan sit in the oven for 1 hour. Cool the seitan in the broth. There is no need to store the seitan in the broth. Store the seitan airtight in the refrigerator for up to 3 days, or freeze for up to two months.

See Recipe Notes, page 169.

YIELD: 6 cutlets (4 ounces, or 113 g each)

Quit-the-Cluck Seitan

▶ SOY-FREE POTENTIAL

This seitan is just as versatile as our Kind-to-Cows Seitan, with a totally different flavor profile. They taste light and slightly herbed. Keep these in the freezer, too, for fast-and-easy meals. This potentially soy-free seitan can be substituted for the Kind-to-Cows Seitan in any of our recipes.

FOR THE SEITAN:

1¼ cups (180 g) vital wheat gluten

¼ cup (32 g) chickpea flour

3 tablespoons (22 g) nutritional yeast

1 tablespoon (7 g) onion powder

2 teaspoons (12 g) dried poultry seasoning

1 teaspoon garlic powder

½ teaspoon ground white pepper

¾ cup (180 ml) vegetable broth, more if needed

2 teaspoons (12 g) vegan bouillon paste, or 2 cubes vegan bouillon, crumbled

1 tablespoon (15 ml) olive oil

1 tablespoon high heat neutral-flavored oil, for cooking

FOR THE COOKING BROTH:

2 cups (470 ml) vegetable broth

1 tablespoon (8 g) nutritional yeast

2 teaspoons (10 g) dried poultry seasoning

2 teaspoons (10 g) onion powder

1 teaspoon Dijon mustard

Salt and pepper

See directions for Kind-to-Cows Seitan, page 168.

Recipe Notes

• If the seitan is shrinking during the rolling, put it on a Silpat to help it retain its shape and size. Let it rest and reroll, as needed.

• For best texture, seitan should be refrigerated (or frozen) before using.

• If any broth is leftover, it can be frozen and used in the next batch of seitan.

• Make this into medallions or nuggets instead! Using 2 teaspoons (15 g) of dough, form into a round patty between your palms. It should be less than ¼-inch (6 mm) thick and about 1½ to 2 inches (3.8 to 5 cm) across. Panfry in batches, then bake as above. You may need an additional tablespoon (15 ml) of oil for cooking. Makes 30 medallions (0.8 ounces, or 23 g each).

• To make braciola (or large cutlets to stuff and roll): Divide the dough into 4 even pieces. Roll out each piece to a 6 x 8 inch (15 x 20 cm) rectangle using the method above. Panfry in batches, and then bake as above, but in a large roasting pan using 3 cups (705 ml) of broth instead of 2 cups (470 ml). The rest of the cooking broth and directions remain the same. Makes 4 braciola-style cutlets (170 g each). If desired, the braciola-style cutlets can be cut into strips or chunks for use in other recipes, as well.

Best Baked Tofu

▶ GLUTEN-FREE POTENTIAL

This savory tofu can be used in a variety of ways: as is, served with gravy, as cutlets in a sandwich, or chopped and made into a no-chicken salad, to name a few. Note: This recipe originally appeared in *The Great Vegan Protein Book* (Steen and Noyes, Fair Winds Press, 2015) and is included here for your convenience.

Nonstick cooking spray

1 pound (454 g) extra-firm tofu, drained, pressed, and cut into ¼-inch (6 mm) thick slices, then cut on the diagonal to form two triangles

½ cup (120 ml) vegetable broth

¼ cup (60 ml) dry white wine, or additional broth

2 tablespoons (15 g) nutritional yeast

1 tablespoon (15 ml) olive oil

2 cloves garlic, minced

1 teaspoon dried poultry seasoning

1 teaspoon vegan bouillon paste (see Recipe Notes)

½ teaspoon onion powder

½ teaspoon fine sea salt

¼ teaspoon garlic powder

Pinch ground white pepper

Spray a 9 x 13-inch (23 x 33 cm) glass baking dish with cooking spray. Stir together the broth through (and including) the white pepper in the baking dish. Add the tofu and turn to coat. Marinate for 1 hour.

Preheat the oven to 400°F (200°C, or gas mark 6). Bake the tofu in the marinade for 20 minutes. Turn the tofu over, and bake for 15 to 20 minutes longer or until golden. The tofu may be baked longer for a firmer consistency, if desired.

YIELD: 1 pound (454 g) tofu

Recipe Notes

- The vegan bouillon paste can be difficult to find. If so, use 2 teaspoons (12 g) dried poultry seasoning and 1 teaspoon salt instead.

- If you'd like to make your own poultry seasoning, combine 1 tablespoon (8 g) nutritional yeast, 2 teaspoons (3 g) dried thyme, 1 teaspoon onion powder, ½ teaspoon dried sage, ½ teaspoon dried rosemary, ½ teaspoon dried marjoram, ½ teaspoon salt, and ½ teaspoon white pepper in a small blender. Process until powdered, and you'll have a generous 2 tablespoons (16 g) of seasoning.

ACKNOWLEDGMENTS

Our endless gratitude goes to our publisher, the Fair Winds dream team, who never fails to make the whole process a perfect blast: Amanda Waddell, Betsy Gammons, Anne Re, Katie Fawkes, and Becky Gissel. Thank you also to Jenna Patton for the stellar copyediting work!

As usual, all of the recipes in this book have gone through rigorous testing before seeing the light of day. We are so grateful to our team of testers for their hard work and dedication: Courtney Blair, Kelly and Mac Cavalier, Shannon Davis, Dorian Farrow, Monique and Michel Narbel-Gimzia, Gary Holliday, Aimee Kluiber, Jenna Patton, Constanze Reichardt, Adam Rosen, Stephanie Sulzman, Jody Weiner, Rochelle Krogar-West, and Liz Wyman.

Warm and fuzzy thanks to those of you who have told a friend about one of our books, left us a review, or prominently placed our books in a store while shopping. Thank you for spreading the vegan word!

ABOUT THE AUTHORS

Celine Steen is the coauthor of *Vegan Sandwiches Save the Day!*, *Whole Grain Vegan Baking*, *The Great Vegan Protein Book*, *The Complete Guide to Even More Vegan Food Substitutions*, and more. She lives in California with her husband and two cats. You can get in touch with her at hello@celinesteen.com.

Tami Noyes is the author of *American Vegan Kitchen* and *Grills Gone Vegan*, and the coauthor of *Vegan Sandwiches Save the Day!* and others. Tami lives outside of Cleveland with her best friend, Jim, and five funny furballs. Follow her blog, veganappetite.com, or email Tami at veganappetite@gmail.com.

INDEX